the doctor is in

the doctor is in

Dr. Ruth on Love, Life, and Joie de Vivre

DR. RUTH K. WESTHEIMER

with Pierre A. Lehu

amazonpublishing

Published by Amazon Publishing, New York

www.apub.com

Amazon, the Amazon logo and Amazon Publishing are
trademarks of Amazon.com, Inc. or its affiliates.

ISBN-10: 1477829601 (hardcover)
ISBN-13: 9781477829608 (hardcover)
ISBN-10: 1477828362 (paperback)
ISBN-13: 9781477828366 (paperback)
eISBN: 9781477878361

Cover design by Laura Klynstra

Library of Congress Control Number: 2014920789

Printed in the United States of America

To all those seeking more joie de vivre in their life

Two are better than one because there is a good reward for their labor.

– Kohelet Ecclesiastes 4:9

TABLE OF CONTENTS

PROLOGUE

The BBC assembled a series of documentaries called *Extraordinary Women* that recently aired around the world, including on many PBS stations in the United States. Each was an hour long, and among the featured women were Indira Gandhi, Grace Kelly, Coco Chanel, Agatha Christie, Audrey Hepburn, Josephine Baker, and me, Dr. Ruth Westheimer. I was very honored to have been included, especially because I was the only one who was still alive. I don't know the particulars of why they chose me, but I guess my life story is one that is rather dramatic, as it's been quite a roller coaster ride: growing up in an Orthodox Jewish family in Frankfurt, Germany, until the age of ten; being put on a *kindertransport* to an orphanage in Switzerland to escape the Holocaust; immigrating at the age of seventeen to Palestine, where I worked on a kibbutz before joining the Haganah, the freedom fighters who trained me to be a sniper; being seriously wounded in a bomb blast on my twentieth birthday; living in Paris for five years; moving to the United States;

and then in my fifties unexpectedly winding up as a world-famous sex therapist.

If the selection process of the series *Extraordinary Women* remains a mystery, I know exactly how the play about my life, *Becoming Dr. Ruth*, came to be written. It all started with an off-Broadway show entitled *Freud's Last Session*. I went backstage and met the actors, including Martin Rayner, who starred as Freud. Later, he called me and asked for a meeting in my office. I wondered if he had a sex problem he wanted some assistance with, but I so enjoyed his performance that I would gladly have tried to help him in any way I could, so we set up the appointment. He came to my office, we chatted a bit, and then he brought up the topic that he'd actually come to see me about.

"Dr. Ruth, you haven't met the playwright of *Freud*, Mark St. Germain, but he's a big fan of yours and he'd like to write a play about your life."

"Martin," I said kindly, "I love the theater, and while it's an interesting proposition, there have already been several documentaries made about my life. So that ground has been covered, and I don't really see this as a viable proposition."

"But, Dr. Ruth," said Martin, playing the role of supplicant almost as well as he did Freud on stage, "Mark is such a talented writer that I'm sure he'd find facets to explore that would be illuminating to audiences."

But delving into the fascinating aspects of my life—such as how it felt to lose my parents or, given my career, revealing the private moments of my sex life—was exactly what I feared. I didn't want Martin to think I'd made a snap judgment after he went to the effort of coming to see me, so I told him I'd think about it. Of course, I didn't have to think about it very much because my mind had pretty much been made up the second I heard the offer. I'd told Martin to have Mark call my minister of communications (and coauthor of this book), Pierre Lehu, and I had Pierre deliver the bad news. Mark then called me, getting my answering machine; he left such a sensitive and sensible message about how much he admired me and that he would never go forward with such a project without my cooperation that almost as fast as I made up my mind when hearing about the idea, I did an about-face and called him back and suggested we meet. We had lunch at Mr. K's, a Chinese restaurant I often go to since it's near my office. In addition to the proximity it offers me, the tables are set far apart so you can have a business lunch while maintaining some privacy. And they have a pair of chopsticks with my name in gold letters!

"Mark," I began, after we'd made some small talk, "I know people are interested in my life history, but I've told those stories over and over."

"But, Dr. Ruth, most people don't know that you were orphaned by the Holocaust or that you were a sniper who fought to create Israel." Mark had done his research, so he knew the basic outlines of my life.

"Perhaps, but there are documentaries that they can watch, or they can look me up on Google if they're really curious."

"What a theatrical piece can do is not only educate people about your history but also bring you, the Dr. Ruth of today, to life. There'll be an actress—I already have somebody in mind—who will portray you, as you are, not just offer up stories about your past."

"And what if I don't like the Dr. Ruth she offers audiences?"

Mark put on his most sincere demeanor—and with his white beard and round face he already projected an honest appearance—and said, "You'll have full approval of the script. If there's anything you don't like, I'll change it. And if you don't like the whole thing, we won't do it. But I have a feeling that you will."

Since the play has already been produced in New York City as well as in the Berkshires, Hartford, Fort Lauderdale and other cities, you know that in the end I agreed. So what got me to change my mind? I've had a very full life, but because there's so much to depict and yet so little material from my past that exists, it's very difficult to show the real me in a documentary. Audiences get a glimpse into my past, and the producers show a lot of stock footage of World War II and Nazis saluting Hitler, and so on. But those early years live only in my memories; there's little to actually show on the screen. In a theatrical production, though, the playwright is free to do as he pleases. He can go back and forth through time so that the audience gets a sense of who I am now, not just who I was back then, and how my past molded the current me. It's that aspect of a theatrical production—at least, one written by as talented a playwright as Mark St. Germain—that made it so enjoyable not only for theater audiences but also for me, which is why I went to see it again and again. I would sit on the edge of my chair watching Debra Jo Rupp. Even though I knew the story better than she did, the way the play jumped back and forth from the past to the play's present kept me riveted.

The first word of the play is "Pierre," as "I'm" on the phone with him. So there's a plot taking place in real time while the actress playing me talks about my life. Debra Jo Rupp, who was the first to portray me and was in the off-Broadway production, did a great job, and we've since become good friends. However, as the play goes to some regional theaters, other actresses will take on this role—and if I can go see them, I will, because I'm very curious to see the differences between them and Debra Jo.

I also enjoy taking part in the overall show by doing what are called Talk Backs after some performances. (I'd done one of those with the cast of *Freud*, and another time I interviewed Martin Rayner answering my questions while he was in character, which we videotaped. You can see it on my YouTube channel.) I love to answer questions from the audience. In these Talk Backs, since the audience has just seen the show and they have a good idea about my life, the questions they ask often manage to surprise me. As you might imagine, sometimes they're not about my life or the play at all, but about that other subject that I specialize in: sex and relationships.

During Talk Backs and in interviews with journalists and the general public, I often get asked: Where do you get your *joie de vivre?* People who learn about my life wonder how I can have so much positive energy. They see that I always appear to be having a good time, and they want to know my secret formula. Of course, there's no one pat answer. I'm not like Popeye the Sailor, opening a can of spinach and ready to take on the world—or at least Bluto. However, it's not accidental. I do make a point of looking on the bright side, and by the time you've finished reading this book, I hope that you'll have some idea of how to get more joy out of your own life. There's no one piece of advice that works for everybody, but I believe life is a little bit like meal preparation. If you take a few ingredients and combine them the right way, you can create something delicious. Two different chefs will come up with slightly different variations, even with the same ingredients; but as long as the end result is pleasing, it doesn't matter. So in each chapter I'll give you some ingredients to try out. Your life won't come out like mine, but maybe you can infuse your life with a little of the *je ne sais pas quoi* that made me go from Karola Ruth Siegel to the one and only Dr. Ruth.

CHAPTER I

What Is Joie de Vivre?

Many moons ago, I lived in Paris for five years. I arrived in Paris a new bride with no knowledge of French, but I left with my second husband (to-be, anyway) speaking French rather well. In French, as in any language, there are phrases that have a special meaning that perhaps can't be perfectly translated (but I will try). *Joie de vivre* literally means "joy of life," but what it really describes are those times when you just feel very alive, your emotions are bursting forth, and you want to skip down the street. It's something you see in little children who squeal with delight at certain times. As adults we learn to squelch those squeals, to hide our emotions, to make every day pretty much the same as the day before. We go through life with our "game face" on, not letting others see the emotions inside of us. The terrible side effect of that is that we are stifling our joie de vivre.

What makes us act that way? Why are we afraid to be joyous? The answer is that it's not so much joy that frightens us but the other emotions, such as sadness and anger. We all have some terrible stories in our past, and in order to keep them buried, we end up stifling all our emotions. And I plead guilty for having done that, though I also had some excuses, as the worst events in my life were truly horrific. The worst one occurred when I was only ten years old.

As a child in Frankfurt I grew up in an Orthodox home. That means we were a bit more stringent in following the religious laws than non-Orthodox Jews, keeping a strictly kosher household, not working on the Sabbath, and going to an Orthodox temple where the men and women prayed in separate sections. Starting around the age of eight, every Friday night I would accompany my father to temple. I don't want to claim any particular religious dedication at that age. I did love being with my father, though, especially because on the way he would buy me ice cream. It had to be before sundown—once the Sabbath began, he couldn't spend any money, so I was like his alarm clock, making sure that we left early enough to make the ice cream stop.

It was unusual for a girl to be sitting next to her father on a Friday night at temple. Such treatment was normally reserved for boys, but as I was an only child, I was allowed to fulfill some of the roles of a son. It's also why I was sent to the Samson Raphael Hirsch School. This was a girl's school, for no Orthodox schools in Germany could be coed, but it was a much-better-thought-of school than the one closer to me. In fact, among my classmates was a Rothschild who was brought to school by a nanny and lived in an enormous mansion. This school was the largest Jewish school in Frankfurt. Most Jewish children went to a Jewish school, in part because Jewish children in public schools were often taunted by young ruffians but also because of the desire to promote Judaism among Jewish children.

While I don't have any memories of being threatened in any way going to and from school, I know that many students were harassed, especially the boys, by groups of young German thugs. Anti-Semitism in Germany was a thread that grew thicker or thinner over hundreds of years of history but never completely snapped, which is one reason that Hitler was able to launch the campaign against Jews so easily. Of course after November 9, 1938, Kristallnacht—or Night of Broken Glass—any semblance of normalcy with regards to the Jews of Frankfurt was destroyed. My school was shut and our synagogue burned down. When Hitler first came to power, my parents had tried to keep their fears from me; now that was impossible. From that night on, I slept in my parents' bed because I didn't want to sleep alone.

My parents put up a brave front—perhaps too brave. Only a week later, on November 15, I was walking with my father on the street in front of our house when a neighbor gave him a stern warning.

"Julius, you must leave Germany as soon as possible, tonight if you can. Things are going to get very bad."

"We might have to leave one day," my father replied, "but tomorrow is a Christian holiday and so for sure we will be safe." But that next morning, two SS storm troopers in their long coats and polished black boots came to our apartment and took my father away.

I have two vivid memories of that morning. First, my grandmother removed some silver coins she had sewn into the hem of her skirt, gave them to one of the SS, and told him to take good care of her son. A lot of good that must have done. And then I rushed to the window and saw my father climb into a truck. I don't know whether or not he could see me, but he looked up toward our windows and smiled, as if to say, "Don't worry, everything will be all right." That was the last time I saw him.

As it turned out, his misfortune was my good fortune. He wasn't taken to a concentration camp; those hadn't been opened yet. He was taken to a detention camp, and eventually he would be sent back, only to perish in a concentration camp later on, along with my mother, paternal grandmother, and maternal grandparents. But because he had been taken away, I became eligible to leave the country. There were *kindertransports*, trains set up to take some German Jewish children out of Germany. In order to get on the list, one of the qualifications was that at least one of your parents had to have been taken away by the Nazis. Thus, because of my father, my mother and grandmother had gotten me a seat on one of those trains bound for Switzerland.

My last memory of my mother and my grandmother is of them running alongside the train I was on as it left the station, waving good-bye. Imitating my father, I gave them a smile, but inside I felt so very lonely and afraid, and once the train pulled out of the station, tears started to stream down my face. I was ten years old, going off to who knows where with one little suitcase and a doll. The doll was my favorite, a celluloid doll. The brand name was Schild-kröte, and it bore the company's unusual trademark on the back that looked like a toad. Sitting across from me was a younger little girl of about five or six who also had tears streaming down her face. She had blond hair and was wearing a little blue dress with white stockings and shiny black shoes, as if she were going to a party. My mother and grandmother had dressed me more sensibly so that I was wearing walking shoes and thick wool socks, as they knew it would be cold up in the mountains where we were headed. Seeing this younger child—who seemed even more vulnerable than me—cry her eyes out changed my attitude. I suddenly grew more concerned for her than for myself. In a moment of generosity (that I readily admit later regretting), I gave her my doll. At first she looked puzzled, but when I insisted that it was now hers, her face lit up with a smile. And at that moment I understood the meaning of the concept of *tzedakah* in Judaism, "giving," which I'd heard spoken about so often in temple. I had given my doll away, but the sense of satisfaction I received from the change in the little girl's face was definitely a reward, and one that I felt counted with God as well.

The impression most people have of me is of this little woman who talks about sex in a funny accent. Some people have an inkling of my past, and some, especially Jews, even know a fair amount about my childhood. But when they see me, they tend to light up with a smile because they know that when Dr. Ruth is in the house, they're going to be tickled by my frank talk and maybe even have a few good laughs. But the question is, how can my head be filled with such sad memories and yet I am still able to make people laugh? It's not always easy, but the secret is to compartmentalize the various sections of your brain. I can put aside the sad memories when I have to, but they're always lurking around somewhere, and sometimes they pop up when I least expect it. The more you practice, the easier it becomes. But to allow the joy to come front and center in your life, you also have to feel your emotions, even the sad ones. You have to mourn, let the tears pour out. If you bottle the sadness in, the joy gets bottled right along with it.

When it comes to having lost my entire family to the Holocaust, one of the most difficult aspects of it for me was that it seemed to take place in slow motion. For a long time I received letters from my family, and I had no idea what fate awaited them. I was betwixt and between, on the one hand believing that we would all be reunited but also fearing that we might not. So I had hope, even though in actuality there was no hope. And then the letters stopped coming. Again, there was no warning. It wasn't as if I got a letter saying there wouldn't be any more posts. No, instead the time between that last letter and the next one that never came just stretched out more and more. As far as I was concerned, the next one was still on its way, and I kept writing letters to them. Why I wasn't getting any answers to my letters was a mystery—what child could have imagined the horrible truth? (In fact, before the Holocaust, I'm not sure many adults could have imagined what the Nazis were doing.) Since I didn't know what had happened, I couldn't really let go. I was in a sort of limbo, an orphan who didn't quite believe my status. And not wanting to believe the truth also clouded my future. That impression—that my parents might one day just show up—haunts me still. It's not a feeling I will ever lose. And yet . . . I haven't clouded my life with this darkness. How do I manage such emotional upheaval with joie de vivre? And how can you do the same with whatever terrible events fill your memory banks?

The answer is to focus on the present. Pay attention to the people around you. Ask questions and listen to the answers. Tell everyone what happened to you during the day and make it as amusing as possible. Accentuate the positive, try to bring everyone's spirits up; by doing that, you'll find your own elevated. And by keeping your brain occupied in the present, it will force toward the back any unpleasant emotions that your past might evoke.

It's easier to manage this if you have the right audience. Some people seem always to be cranky and tired, and I don't have the time or space in my life for such types. Sadly, sometimes this pattern develops in old age. One reason that young people often keep a safe distance from older people is that many past a certain age have lost their zest for life. All they seem to do is complain about their aches and pains, how expensive everything is, and that their kids haven't called. That's not to say that old age doesn't bring with it much to complain about; but entering a particular age bracket shouldn't mean that a cloud of gloom has to permanently descend over you. However, even if you are with a lot of older adults, you can change the atmosphere if you put enough energy into it.

Here is a prime example. Every so often I go on a cruise ship for a few days. I don't go on the whole cruise. I jump on the boat at some port, stay a few days, give some lectures, and then I'm off the boat and flying to wherever I want to go in that part of the world. It's the free travel that draws me to these offers, not the part where you sit in a deck chair only to get up to hit the dining room. Yes, I do eat while on board the ship so in a sense I'm singing for my supper, but really I'm talking for my ticket.

My only duty is to give a lecture or two. If I wanted, I could sit in my cabin the rest of the time and the cruise line would be happy with me. But I wouldn't be. I enjoy meeting new people, so I roam around the ship, and when someone says "Dr. Ruth!" I start talking to them. And yes, many of them are retired, though the very fact that they're on a cruise instead of sitting at home staring at each other means they have the potential for joie de vivre—and may even be actively seeking it. If I run into some people who are complaining nonstop, well, that's why I always make sure that I get a cabin with a terrace so that if I feel the need to get away and just read by myself for a while, I have someplace to go.

I enjoy hearing about what people do when they're not on that cruise ship. One reason is my natural curiosity; to me it's also a bit like going treasure hunting. If you speak to enough people on a cruise ship, at a charity fund-raiser, at an opening-night gala, or sitting next to you in first class on an airplane, you're bound to meet a few people who have the wherewithal to help you in some way. In my case, maybe they have a lot of money that they can contribute to one of my favorite charities. Or else they may be involved in a business that complements a project I'm working on. So if there's even a whiff of money in the air, I never waste an opportunity to see if I can make a useful connection.

But if I'm looking to get something a little extra from going on these cruises, I also offer something a little extra back. On any cruise I'm on, I make a point of giving a special lecture just for the crew. This is not asked of me; it's something that I arrange with the captain once I'm on board. It's usually done rather late at night, when most of the passengers are in bed and the crew has some free time. Since this is such a rare occurrence for the crew, they really enjoy themselves, and that festive atmosphere in turn gives me so much enjoyment. It's not that the passengers aren't there to have fun—but sometimes you have to pull it out of them. People who are always taking cruises can become a little blasé. But the crew goes wild when they hear me talking about sex with the captain at my side (usually a little red in the face), and that makes my spirits soar.

I was once invited on the Love Boat. It was a special anniversary and the actor who played the captain on the television show, Gavin MacLeod, was also on board. All the passengers were gathered on the deck, and we both spoke to them. When it was my turn, I gave them my usual type of homework.

"When we're done here, I want you all to go back to your cabins and try a new position."

The crowd roared, but then the captain had to interrupt: "Hold on, if you all start rocking the boat at the same time, the boat's going to sink."

"OK," I said, "so we'll do one deck at a time. Let's start in the middle with Deck Three!"

Did anyone actually try a new position? Who knows! People did later report to me that they had a good time, either in words, winks, or smiles. My little talk gave them permission to have sex, and that's what mattered. Not that they went on a cruise to be celibate; but if a couple is having sex the same way over and over again at home, there's a good chance they'll have the same type of sex on board a ship. However, if they're going to their cabin in the middle of the afternoon with homework from Dr. Ruth, that might give them just the push they need to try something a little different—and so share in some of my joie de vivre.

∾

Another way of avoiding the trap of being surrounded by miserable people is to make sure that you cultivate good friends who know how to lift your mood, or at least don't fight you when you try to lift theirs. I have one friend, Dr. David Best, who is several decades younger than me, but more important than his age is that he shares the same philosophy of making the most out of life. For example, he makes sure to attend every Olympics. It's not your usual hobby, and it sure has taken him to some unusual places, but it always gives him something to look forward to, even four years down the road.

In addition to building on his perfect attendance record at the Olympics, David's also a dog lover. He has a Jack Russell terrier that he named Elvis who is with him almost all the time, including at the office. Now, lots of people love their dogs, but David can go to extremes. For example, when Elvis was whatever age equals thirteen in dog years, David threw him a "bark mitzvah" at a Jewish restaurant in lower Manhattan. When I got the invitation, I was a bit taken aback because this whole concept is a little sacrilegious, though I know David isn't the first one to do it. But David's a good friend, and he of course wanted my presence there. This was one of those invitations that couldn't be turned down.

There were at least a hundred of us crowded into the top-floor dining room, stuffing ourselves with a variety of Jewish delicacies like pastrami and potato latkes. Elvis was greeting everybody, as was his birth mother, whom David had invited down from upstate New York. (I'm glad no one from the Department of Health showed up, or the guest of honor and his mom would have had to be escorted out.) David is always putting together funny films, most of which feature Elvis, so of course there was a video to watch of Elvis making a trip to Jerusalem to prepare for his big day. And then there was the ceremony itself. No rabbi—but Elvis was escorted in by several robotic dogs bearing sparklers. The entire evening was totally over the top, but I got into the spirit of it. I'd brought doggie chew toys in the shape of Jewish items like a dreidel, and though a part of me would cringe every once in a while as I watched my religion (and David's) get trampled on, I also had a great time, especially dancing to the Jewish music.

Adapting a positive attitude is a vital part of my joie de vivre philosophy. If you're going to show up at an event, make the most of it. That might mean diving in to everything that's going on, or it might be finding that one interesting person and maneuvering him or her into a corner for some good conversation. As long as you take away something from being there, then all is not lost and you can look back at the evening as having been a good one. So don't just go with the flow. Instead, pour some of your energy into wherever you are so that the outcome is a positive one.

One day David called and said we had to get together; he had something serious to discuss. He was having a hard time making a decision, and he wanted my advice. Of course, it had to do with Elvis. You might think that if he could decide to do a bark mitzvah without consulting me, he didn't need my advice for anything else Elvis-related. But this time my doctor friend was definitely indecisive.

"There's going to be a reality television series that features owners and their dogs. The producers saw the video I made of the bark mitzvah on YouTube, and they've asked me and Elvis to be contestants."

"So what's the problem?" I asked, picturing Elvis on national TV becoming more famous than me (and not liking the idea!).

"It's being filmed in California, and if Elvis and I don't get voted off right away, we could be out there for weeks—and I have a business to run." Though David is a medical doctor, he gave up practicing medicine years ago in order to pursue a career in medical marketing.

"How much can you win?" was the question that popped into my mind.

"A hundred thousand dollars."

"Then go. First of all, if you didn't go, you'd always regret it. And if you stay till the end, you might win a hundred thousand dollars. And either way, you and Elvis get to be on national TV. And if you win, for helping you decide, I want my ten percent!"

I would have given my share to charity, but as it turned out, Elvis is not a very disciplined pet; he and David were quickly out of the running. However, David then milked Elvis's temporary fame for all it was worth, and he became a mini-celebrity here in New York. That's an example of joie de vivre.

I know that David would have gone without my advice. What he wanted was my permission to leave his business for potentially quite some time. I'm used to that, because it happens to me often. People ask me questions, but they don't really want an answer. They want me to give my blessing to something that might be a little sketchy, like having a threesome. If they knew me better, they'd know that I'm going to tell them to keep their pants on—but I let them ask because if I can keep even some of these people from taking risks with their marriage, I'll have done a good job.

~

Truly, joie de vivre is about embracing the best ways to enjoy life. Let me hit you with another French word, *blasé*. Blasé leads to the opposite of joie de vivre. Instead of being amazed, you are always bored. Every year during the holidays, I go to Fifth Avenue to admire the displays in the department store windows and stare up at the tree at Rockefeller Center with wonder. If I can get an invitation, I even go to the tree-lighting ceremony no matter how cold it may be. I also make a point of going to the Macy's Thanksgiving Day Parade every year. Because I'm Dr. Ruth, more often than not I get to sit in the reviewing stand. And no matter how many times I've gone, I always look forward to it. These aren't exclusive events reserved for the rich and famous; these sights and sounds are available to anyone. But to enjoy them you have to have almost a childlike vision. You have to see them as if you are seeing them for the first time in order to feel the excitement they can offer. If you go and complain about the cold and say to yourself, "What's the big deal?"—if you're going to be blasé—then your life is going to be boring.

A common question I get is: "Dr. Ruth, how do I keep boredom from creeping into our sex life?" The type of answer people expect from me is, "Turn to page so and so of the Kama-sutra," or "Cover yourselves in whipped cream." I'm all for adding variety to one's sex life, but that in and of itself will not cure sexual boredom because the main cause isn't having sex in a repetitive manner but rather boredom with the entire relationship. If, when you look across at your partner while having breakfast, you say to yourself "Boring," then you won't be any less bored if you're naked on the floor in the Tominagi position.

The real answer to that question is to work hard at kicking boredom out of every aspect of the relationship. So if one or both of you are always blasé, always belittling whatever it is you're doing rather than finding ways to share the excitement in it, then your relationship is pretty much doomed unless something changes. The best advice I can give you is to figure out how you can go through life with your eyes and mouth wide open with excitement. And don't worry—it's OK if you drool a bit!

CHAPTER II

Always Move Forward

B ecause I'm only four foot seven, I'm naturally drawn to the
concept that those of us who make any contributions to society
only do so by standing on the shoulders of giants. For me, among the
giants are those who first began to research human sexual function-
ing, such as Alfred Kinsey, Masters and Johnson, and Helen Singer
Kaplan, who trained me. But my upward climb toward becoming
a sex therapist started a lot more modestly, and rather than giants,
I had to stand on a wobbly precipice of my own creation, two dark
mahogany dining room chairs that I put one on top of the other and
then proceeded to scale.

I was ten years old at the time, living in Frankfurt, Germany.
My life revolved around my parents, Julius and Irma Siegel, and
my paternal grandmother, Selma, whose home we lived in. I didn't
know much about sex, but I'd picked up enough information from
whispered comments, body language, and even some strange noises
I'd hear at night to make me curious. While most of my parents'
books were neatly arranged on a couple of bookshelves in the living

room, there was one that my parents kept secreted away from me in a locked cabinet on a shelf on top of a closet. If I'm short now, I was even shorter then—but I knew where the key was . . . and on an afternoon when I was left alone for a while, I decided to play Eve and take a bite out of that apple.

I put together my climbing contraption, risked life and limb to clamber up to the top of the closet, and retrieved the tome. It was titled *Ideal Marriage;* I later learned that it was written by a man named Van de Velde and was the classic "marriage manual" of the period. I skipped the parts that were of no interest to me—such as the art of conversation—and zeroed in on the chapter about sex, which stood out because of the drawings of various positions. Now at least I could picture what was going on, though at that age it didn't really mean all that much to me except that like all forbidden fruit, I knew it was something I wanted to learn more about. However, I didn't get to spend much time educating myself because I heard my parents at the door. I quickly returned the book to its rightful place, thinking I would have another opportunity to look at it more closely. Because of the Holocaust, I never got the chance to see that book again, nor did I get "the talk" from my parents. So, as it turned out, when it came to sex, those few stolen moments with that book had to do as my educational foundation. At least, until I learned more firsthand.

Of course, the Nazis curtailed my education in many more ways than just keeping me in the dark about sex. The Swiss Jews who ran the school where I wound up didn't consider German refugees worthy of a real education. They seemed to be under the impression that in exchange for providing a roof over our heads and three meals a day, we had to perform as the dutiful caretakers of the Swiss Jewish children in that boarding school. That's why instead of a high school diploma I have a degree in Swiss housekeeping, which I proudly display at the bottom of a closet. My dreams of becoming a medical doctor evaporated in the fumes of the cleaning fluids that I used daily to clean the school's toilets.

I did manage to get some education during the six years I spent in Heiden, but only by being resourceful. The refugee boys attended actual school classes, as back in those days men weren't considered good housemaid material. Since we German refugees stuck together, and I particularly stuck to one boy nicknamed Putz, I was able to borrow his school textbooks. I didn't always understand what I was reading—particularly in math—but I was determined not to let the education I normally would have been given during these years slip entirely away. Just before curfew, Putz would hand over a textbook or two that I'd take with me to bed to pore over using a flashlight.

During the periods when I was madly in love with Putz, this system worked. However, there were times when Putz got on my nerves. For example, I once wrote in my diary that he refused to part his hair to the side as I requested—so as far as I was concerned, Putz and I were kaput. But whatever the status of our relationship, I still managed to pick up enough material to keep me from being a complete ignoramus.

~

One of my secrets to getting the most from life is that I naturally forget bad things that happen to me. That's not to say I don't hold grudges. However, if I've forgotten why I should be holding that grudge, it slips through my fingers, along with all the bad vibrations that come with anything negative. This forgetfulness when it comes to negative incidents isn't something that's happened to me in old age, so don't go thinking it's senility (though I'm no stranger to "senior moments"). I've always been like that, which is probably why I've been able to attend the Frankfurt Book Fair so many times. No, I haven't forgotten what the Nazis did. But if I were to completely cut myself off from Germany, I wouldn't be getting back at Hitler. He didn't want me to grow up or even survive in Germany. He committed suicide; meanwhile, I'm living life to the fullest, even from time to time in the city from which I had to flee. Granted, I wouldn't buy a German-made car because I don't want to be reminded of what happened every time I climb into it. But while I had to steel myself the first few times I went to Germany, I taught myself to move on. You can't experience joie de vivre if you're carrying around a huge lump of bitterness.

When I was asked to be the grand marshal of the Steuben Parade here in New York—a celebration by German Americans—I paused once again to decide whether or not it was appropriate to accept this honor. You'll find me at every Israel Day Parade, not to mention the Macy's Thanksgiving Day Parade, so it wasn't as if I were suffering from some sort of parade deficit. And there was no doubt that for me to lead this particular parade was something that some members of the Jewish community wouldn't understand. But to not accept was like saying that all Germans are inherently evil. As a Jew who actively stands against anti-Semitism, how could I refuse based on the same sort of logic that I so despise? So I marched at the head of that parade and had a fabulous time.

It was a gorgeous sunny September day. They'd placed a picture of me on flags attached to the lampposts all along Fifth Avenue, and it gave me a big smile each time we walked by one. Plus I had two police detectives assigned to me the whole time. They'd picked me up at home, and on the drive to the start of the parade, I had them put the siren on their unmarked car. (Shhh—don't tell the police commissioner or they might get into trouble.) I walked up Fifth Avenue, with the expensive apartment buildings on one side and Central Park on the other; thousands of people were waving at me and calling out, "Dr. Ruth, Dr. Ruth!" I waved back, checking out the crowds on both sides in case I should spot someone I know.

When we arrived at the reviewing stand, I was actually a little sad to stop walking, as it meant an end to the accolades I was getting.

Imagine missing out on an opportunity to receive such an out-pouring of admiration because of events that took place seventy years before. The passing years don't diminish what happened in the least, but if the people honoring me weren't even born, they certainly played no role. And if we are to prove Hitler wrong—that no race is superior or inferior—then we have to treat everyone equally, and that goes for all the German people born since World War II.

I am also on very friendly terms with the Swiss community here in New York. The last three Swiss counsel generals have invited me to the official residence many times, either just for dinner or to attend a concert they're hosting. And I'm a regular at the annual Swiss Ball, at which a good part of the community gets together to celebrate their heritage. Again, my feelings toward the Swiss are mixed. On the one hand, they saved my life, and I will always be grateful for that. But I can't help to think of all the other German Jewish children whom they weren't willing to take, and I wasn't treated very well while I was there (and this was by Swiss Jews, no less). When the war was over, I was forced to leave. I don't know that I would have wanted to stay, but the decision wasn't mine to make. We were refugees, and now that the fighting was over, we were expressly told that the time had come to go elsewhere. But if the Swiss want to treat me like a celebrity today, then why not enjoy myself? There's that expression, "to cut off your nose to spite your face," and not accepting the welcome I'm given today by the Swiss because I wasn't allowed to attend classes in the 1940s would be a prime example of that. Plus, I go to Switzerland almost as often as I go to Israel. Mostly it's because I have some dear friends who live there, but also, hiking in the Swiss Alps is a favorite of mine—not to mention Swiss chocolates! While it's one thing to have a good time with Germans or Swiss, though, nothing compares to celebrating with my fellow

Jews, especially those who were with me in Switzerland. When we get together—and we're all rather old now—and we spend hours dancing to traditional Israeli folk songs, what's showing through is our joie de vivre. Because each of us came close to dying along with the rest of our families, we all have this drive to make the most of the days we have left. Compare us to the usual high school reunion and you have joie de vivre in 3-D surround sound.

One reason for our cohesion is that we had a common enemy. Everyone has a teacher who was universally disliked, but we had Fraulein Riesenfeld, who surpasses those others in just about every way. On the first day we arrived in Heiden, I watched as she stole the chocolate bar my grandmother had placed in my suitcase. She told us that once we went upstairs to bed, we couldn't come back down. The bathroom was downstairs, and knowing you couldn't go to the bathroom made the need to go that much worse. So, of course, several times I wet the bed, as did others. Not only did she embarrass us in front of the other children by making us wash our sheets, but she then ordered us to write about it to our parents. But far worse than any of her day-to-day cruelty, she actually told us—not just me, but all the children—that our parents were snakes, animals who eat their young, because they'd sent us away. Can you get any meaner? (One time I saw her slip on the ice. I laughed and laughed. I got spanked, but it was well worth it.)

When you've shared being under the domination of someone like Fraulein Riesenfeld, with no place to go for relief, no loving family to turn to, if nothing else it builds a sense of community. We couldn't turn to our parents, so we turned to each other. We created bonds that were tough enough to last a lifetime. But when we get together, we aren't bitter. We don't cry about what happened. Instead we find ways of making each other laugh. Once you learn to squeeze some fun out of what really are sour lemons, that's a skill you never lose. You learn not to dwell on what's horrible in your life because you've come face-to-face with real horror and know that's a place you don't want to revisit. You look for the good that life has to offer rather than make petty complaints.

Of course, I wasn't alone in that school/orphanage in Heiden. Is there maybe something in my genetic code that made me stand out from all the other children there? That's a good question—and believe it or not, I have an answer to it, because I wondered the same thing myself. For my master's dissertation at the New School, I did a study of the other children who were with me. Several years later, with the help of a famous Swiss journalist, I did more digging, which eventually turned into my first book, *Die Geschichte der Karola Siegel* (*The Story of Karola Siegel*). I'm not going to go into detail of what was written in that book, as you're already in the middle of another of my books, but I confirmed the basic point that because all of us had come from loving, solid families before Hitler came to power, we'd all been given a solid foundation on which to grow into useful and productive citizens. Despite becoming orphans and having to survive some tough years in Heiden, none of us dropped out of society or became addicts. We all were able to create and support families of our own. Our roots had taken hold, and we were all able to overcome the hardships of those years—perhaps scarred, but not terminally damaged.

That's not to say that there aren't plenty of successful people whose very early life started out in substandard conditions, but who despite their past were able to pull themselves up by those proverbial bootstraps. The difference between them and our group is that they were the exceptions; many of those around them were not able to overcome those initial disadvantages. But I wasn't the exception of our own group (OK, most didn't become famous but that's not how I define success). Rather, we all managed to thrive after the war ended.

The lesson that I want you to draw from this is that if you had a strong foundational childhood, then you too have a background on which you can draw enormous strength. If you're facing a problem, don't tell yourself that you can't do it. Convince yourself that you have the strength to deal with almost anything because of the way you were raised. And you do! Recognizing your core strengths is an important step toward having joie de vivre. You can count on better days to come because of the good days that came before. And you can find joy in the moment because you have the resiliency to overcome the problems that may be hanging over you.

~

Another side of my life that has played a strong role is faith. Yes, there's religious faith, but here I'm talking about faith in yourself. If your background didn't provide you with the solid foundation that those of us in Heiden had been given by our families, you still need a foundation to hang on to, and in such cases you have to make it yourself. You have to believe that you have the abilities to get ahead. That's not to say that there won't be days when that faith is shaken, because it will be. When you fail badly, you'll wonder if you have what it takes. But you have to learn how to bounce back.

When I was severely wounded—a story we'll get to—I wasn't certain I'd ever walk again. But I forced myself to find the courage that I needed. One of my motivations was that I'd lost my family and it was my duty to carry on. Was I actually under any pressure to succeed on their behalf? Of course not; they were gone from this earth. But I used that logic to rally my forces. So if you can't find a foundation to lean on in the obvious places, such as your immediate family, then come up with another. It could be religion, it could be other relatives, a favorite teacher, your country, your race—the possibilities are endless. By convincing yourself that you're not acting alone, no matter how lonely you may feel, you'll be able to find the strength you need through this faith you've developed. If you don't believe me, think of all the soldiers who've run headfirst into battle, risking their lives to protect their country. Their faith gave them the necessary courage. You too can find a similar source of faith to get you through dark times.

CHAPTER III

Embrace Your Passions and Your Beliefs

There was a time when America's most famous celebrities hid their Jewish origins, people such as Kirk Douglas (born Issur Danielovitch) or Lauren Bacall (born Betty Joan Perske). And some still do today—or at least, they keep it quiet, as they feel that being part of the Jewish minority might hinder a career in show business. But my career goals never were to be a celebrity; the only reason I dropped my last name (to the extent that I go by Dr. Ruth instead of Dr. Ruth Westheimer) was because people had a hard time remembering it and saying it on radio. I have always been very proud of being Jewish. I certainly suffered enough for my religious beliefs that for me, to try to hide being Jewish would have done nothing more than hand a partial victory to Hitler. So the fact that I am Jewish does not come as a surprise to most people. But my past does contain some surprises. What's the biggest one? German—not a surprise. Grandmother—not a surprise. Sniper—definitely a surprise!

When it was time to leave Switzerland, I had to decide where to relocate. Did I want to go back to Germany? After what had happened there, absolutely not. But if my parents or other family members were possibly alive, I knew beyond every shadow of doubt the first thing they would do is come look for me. And where would they start searching? One logical place was back in Frankfurt. That's where they last saw me, and potentially they had belongings there. If I were them, that's where I would have gone. So if I moved anywhere else but Frankfurt, how would they find me? Granted, by this time I knew enough about the Holocaust that the odds of them being alive were small. But these were my parents; even the smallest odds were something to hold on to. So what should have been a relatively easy decision—to go to Palestine—in fact became gut wrenching. To some degree, my decision made me feel like I was abandoning my family. Wasn't my duty to return to the apartment where we had lived and wait for them to possibly show up? My only consolation was that Palestine was probably the second place they'd look for me. But still, as I made my way there, the thought that this move might mean never seeing my parents or grandparents again weighed heavily on me.

When I got to Palestine, I was told in no uncertain terms that I had to give up my German first name, Karola. Anything German was considered tainted, and it didn't matter that it was the name my dear parents had given me. But if my parents were looking for me and thought of looking in Palestine, how would they find me if I changed my name? I arrived at half a solution, inverting my first and middle names, becoming Ruth Karola from Karola Ruth, rationalizing that it would make it easier for my parents to locate me. But the truth was that with this gesture, I was not just losing the identity I'd had for my entire life; I was also lessening the chances that any of my family might ever find me. So now I was adding a layer of guilt to what was already a painful exercise of becoming Ruth.

All these thoughts would never have occurred to me if I'd had some remains or a cemetery plot to visit. Not having that type of evidence left me with an open wound that never completely healed. I still sometimes dream of finding my parents. My experience allows me to better understand the emotions of the families of those who perished in 9/11 and other tragedies, where no remains are ever found. That hope—that maybe your loved one escaped, is maybe in a hospital in a coma, or lost his or her memory and is living a new life—always remains. Mourning is an important human activity for restoring mental health, in every sense of the phrase. Those of us who can't fully experience these emotions have a hard time coming fully to grips with the loss.

Each of us in the orphanage dealt with this loss in a different way. I witnessed one example of that with a boy that I liked, Walter (aka Putz), when he was ordered into the office of the evil Fraulein Riesenfeld. Knowing she'd be up to no good and seeing that the door was slightly ajar, I stood outside listening and watching.

"Walter, we have gotten word that there is a record of your parents being sent to Buchenwald. They are not among the survivors." Walter said nothing. He looked past Fraulein Riesenfeld, and then he started to laugh. He laughed harder and harder until Fraulein Riesenfeld slapped him. I'd had enough at that point. I pushed the door open and ran in, shouting, "Don't touch him! I got a letter from my father! He and my mother and grandmother are safe in Tel Aviv! My father has a job on a farm! We have a little house all to ourselves! Walter can come with me! Everyone can come with me!"

Fraulein Riesenfeld burst that balloon, snarling at me, "Karola, I never read that letter." It wasn't a serious fantasy of mine. I'd made it up on the spur of the moment because seeing Walter laugh like that made me instinctively want to protect him. But as much as I wanted to offer him a life preserver at that moment, the truth was that we were all drowning in our sorrow.

Many of us headed to Palestine. When I first arrived there, I worked on a kibbutz for a time, then went to Jerusalem to learn to be a kindergarten teacher. Then the War of Independence broke out in 1948, and we Jews were at risk of losing our homeland. I wasn't about to let that happen, so I volunteered for the underground. There were several such paramilitary groups, but the largest was the Haganah, which is the one I joined.

As a four-foot-seven woman, I would have been turned away by any self-respecting army anywhere else in the world, but there weren't very many Jews in Palestine at that time (or anywhere, for that matter, given what the Nazis had done to our people). And there were a lot of Arabs in the countries all around us looking to prevent a Jewish state from forming. So it was all hands on deck, even those for whom it was tough to find what might pass for a uniform that fit. Though my sex and size might not have qualified me, it turns out I had other qualities that made me a valuable guerrilla.

The first thing I was taught was how to take apart and put back together a machine gun with my eyes closed. I'm not sure how useful a skill that is, though I suppose if your gun jams during a fight in the middle of the night, you'd be glad to know what to do. In any case, I became quite proficient—it was drilled into me so strongly that if you placed one of those guns in my hands today, I bet I could do it all over again, though I might have to cheat and pull the blindfold aside.

They gave us some training in how to shoot and then I was sent out to the range and handed a rifle that was about as big as I was. It wasn't all that easy to handle standing up, but I was instructed to lie on my belly in the hot sand and fire at a target hundreds of yards away. I was fumbling around, trying to find the right position to align my eye with the gun's sight, when the instructor came up behind me.

"Siegel, what's the problem?"

"I can't find a comfortable position," I said, squirming around on the ground like a dog looking to find just the right orientation to begin a nap.

"Maybe I could bring you a pillow? The Haganah has a large supply. Above all, we want our fighters to be comfy."

"I'm trying very hard, but I've never done this before," I said, feeling a little sorry for myself.

"Here, let me give you something better than target out there? Pretend Adolf Hitler is stand heart is right where the red circle is. See if t

And it did. My emotional state c ad of wallowing in misery, I felt a surge of adrena I had my chance to get even with the man who had destroyed my family, even if it was only inside my head. The rifle scope hurt my cheek and the sand was getting inside my blouse, but I didn't care. I aimed, squeezed the trigger slowly as I had been taught, and fired off five bullets. And they all went into that red circle!

It turned out that I have a knack for putting bullets exactly where I want them to go. It's not like I had practiced playing cowboys and Indians back in Frankfurt, but for some reason, if you put a gun in my hands and a target in front of me, I'll drill those bullets right through the middle of it. And I have never lost that talent. I once took my grandson Ari to a country fair. He challenged my stories about having been a sniper as we stood in front of one of those shooting galleries where you can win prizes if you hit the target—though few do, because it's a lot harder than it looks. We came home with a dozen stuffed animals and a goldfish in a plastic bag full of water. My daughter was annoyed with me because she didn't know where she would put all my winnings!

While I would certainly have been more than willing to take aim at Hitler in real life, I'm actually thankful that I never had to shoot anyone. The main duty that was assigned to me was to stand up on the roof of a building and oversee a checkpoint down below. If anyone tried to force their way through, I would have had to put my shooting skills to the test. Only once while I was on duty did someone forget the password. Seeing that there was a problem, I picked up my rifle and unlatched the safety. But suddenly the man in question regained the use of his tongue, the password slipped out, and I put the safety back on my gun.

In addition to standing on rooftops ready to shoot enemy invaders, I also served as a messenger. I was fast—and I guess because I was short, those in charge must have figured that I would make a small target for the other side's snipers. No one ever said that to me, but when I was delivering messages, I kept my legs moving and made sure to stay as low to the ground as I could, because if they were using me to deliver a message, that meant there was an element of risk.

I didn't serve very long in the Haganah. My tour was cut short after I was seriously wounded, though it had nothing to do with my duties as a sentry or messenger. It was my twentieth birthday, June 4, 1948. I was in the youth hostel where I was living while studying to be a kindergarten teacher, which I continued to do while also serving in the Haganah. Air raid sirens went off that afternoon, which meant we had to go down to the shelter in the basement. The shelter was a big room lined with benches and lit by candles. Since this was a fairly common occurrence, I wasn't overly worried. From experience I knew that we might be sitting down there for some time. A friend had given me a novel in Hebrew for my birthday; I decided to run up to my room, grab the book, and then head down to the shelter. I was walking through the lobby on my way to the basement stairs when a shell landed right outside the front door, sending shrapnel in every direction. There was plaster and blood everywhere as dust rained down from the ceiling. Three people died, including a girl standing right next to me. I was thrown up against the wall, though I don't have any recollection of exactly how that happened. While I had pieces of shrapnel embedded all over, the worst pain came from my legs. I looked at them, and my friend Hannelore was trying to unlace the new shoes I had gotten for my birthday. I was stunned and wondered why she was doing that. Once she'd removed them, I could see all the blood. I said to her, "Do I have to die?"

I was feeling very woozy. Whether it was from the loss of blood or the fear that I might never walk again, I don't know, but when the ambulance arrived and I was put on a stretcher, rather than give in to the feeling of losing consciousness, I forced myself to remain alert. I knew a doctor at Hadassah Hospital, so that's where I wanted to be taken.

"Take me to Hadassah Hospital," I demanded of the ambulance driver.

"What do you think this is, a taxi service? I take you where I'm told."

"But I have a dear friend there," I pleaded. "He is a doctor, and he will look after me."

The driver hesitated, and I knew then that if I pressed him further, I would get my way.

"I'm an orphan of the Holocaust. If I'm going to die, I don't want to die alone. At least at Hadassah Hospital I'll have a friendly face to look at."

I don't like playing the Holocaust card, but I was desperate, and it worked. The only problem was that my doctor friend wasn't on duty when I arrived, and I had so many pieces of shrapnel in me and was bleeding so much that I couldn't wait around for him to show up. By using his name, though, I got a surgeon friend of his to take my case. I had a fairly large piece of shrapnel in my neck, which thankfully hadn't pierced an artery or I never would have made it. I'd also lost the top of my right foot, but the surgeon did a wonderful job of piecing me back together. (Once everything healed, I was back to dancing and later skiing. And no, the surgery isn't why I'm so short!)

Bodies were coming into the hospital at quite a pace. I was sent to another part of the hospital, which was a former cloister being used for convalescence. The building was packed with wounded soldiers and civilians. Since I was afraid of another bombing attack, when they brought me in, I pleaded with the admitting nurse to be put in the basement, which had been the library. I was told there were no available beds, but I got pretty worked up about my fear of another bomb blast. Luckily for me, the nurse was not only willing to bend the rules a bit but was also creative. It was true that there wasn't a single empty bed in the basement, but noting my size, she ordered that I be placed on top of a bookshelf, where I just fit.

There must have been fifty wounded soldiers down there, some very seriously hurt and who wouldn't make it. But the morale was pretty good, considering, and the conditions were certainly uplifting to my morale, as I was the only woman in the room. That got me a lot of attention, and I loved it. Not only was I being noticed by all these soldiers, but there was also a very handsome male nurse who seemed to be spending a lot of time at my side. He had started medical school in Romania but hadn't been able to finish. He was tall with dark blond hair and a twinkle in his eye. During a truce period, when there were no bombings, he came up to me with a special surprise as I lay there on my bookshelf.

"Ruth, I think some sunshine would be good for you. What do you think?"

"How do I get outside?" I asked, looking into his pale blue eyes.

"Like this," he said, as he picked me up in his arms. He carried me all the way into the courtyard and lay me down on some pillows that he'd placed ahead of time on the ground. I have to say, as a method of transportation, that one can't be beat. He did that every day for the rest of the week—and believe me, I enjoyed every second of each trip and let him know it. I must have gotten my message across, because a few weeks later, when I was back at the hostel, he contacted me and we had a brief but intense love affair.

Despite being wounded—or maybe a little because of it—I am very proud that I took an active role in the creation of Israel. However,

I was always a little disappointed that I never got any recognition for it. Then, in the summer of 2013 while I was in Israel, I received a commendation. Better late than never? Absolutely. Not that anyone ever doubted my story; it is a bit too outrageous to be a lie.

I don't recommend fighting a war to anyone, but the feeling of being on the same side when the game involves not a ball but real bullets definitely brings you closer to your friends. On the larger scale, you're serving your country; but when it comes to your unit, you're actually defending each other's lives. You depend on the other members of your unit, and they depend on you. It's a unique feeling. We children had felt it to some degree when it came to Fraulein Riesenfeld, but as nasty an individual as she was, she could threaten only our bottoms, not our lives.

When you're in danger, you can't help but take advantage of any break in the action. I know people in the business world are under a lot of stress, but try running down an alleyway knowing you might get shot at any moment. Now that's stressful! So when you're not on duty, the relief you feel is palpable. It might not be the joy of life so much as the joy of being alive, but it definitely gives you an appreciation of life that's hard to get anywhere else.

For your sake, I hope you never have to experience such circumstances. But if you want to feel joie de vivre in your everyday life, paying attention to your feelings when you are in a tight situation is a useful exercise. If you're driving with your partner and you have a narrow miss, acknowledge the close call, touch each other, and if it's safe, look at each other. When you're out of the car, give each other a hug like you really mean it. Maybe imagine the worst for a second so that the person in your arms feels more special for that brief encounter. Joie de vivre isn't limited to the best of times; it can also be felt in the worst of them. One of the most important guiding principles that I take from Judaism is the concept of *tikkun olam*, "repairing the world." No one is immune from tragedy; everyone endures moments in life that are sad and hard to overcome. I'm not trying to make you feel extra sorry for me, because when all is said and done, my life turned out pretty well. But what happened to me and so many other survivors of the Holocaust was that our entire world got ripped to shreds. Even the survivor of a tornado who can see nothing but destruction all around still has a larger society to fall back on. He or she remains an American from a certain state and has friends and family nearby. Those of us sent to the school in Heiden had none of that. We had to start from scratch to build a new world for ourselves. And so more than most, we understand how important it is to keep the world we have in good repair. We Jews do that through *mitzvahs*, good deeds. No one person can do it all, but if each of us tries to do our part, we can make our contribution. And so if I have been able to help others enjoy their sexuality more, I take that as part of my contribution to *tikkun olam*.

While I have maintained my Judaism, I'm no longer Orthodox. I don't believe that I have to strictly obey one set of rules to prove my faith, though I respect those who do. But I don't belong to only one synagogue. One reason is that if anybody wonders why I wasn't at synagogue last week, they think I was at the other! And in truth I go to many synagogues in New York, as I'm invited to Shabbat services all the time and have many rabbis and cantors whom I count as good friends.

Being a celebrity in a house of worship is a little strange. You're there to humble yourself before God, yet it's difficult to feel sufficiently humble when you hear people whispering behind you, "Look, it's Dr. Ruth." It's at times like these that I'm glad I became famous later in life. If you're a young person in the spotlight, there are a lot more temptations. I can have fun being Dr. Ruth and at the same time take a step back and lean on my past to keep both my feet on the ground. And part of that support system is most definitely my religion.

There are some people who use religion to kill joie de vivre. They've reached the conclusion that anything that is joyful should be put aside and that the only pleasure people should find is in worship. I guess you could say they have joie de religion. My advice to such people is to read the Song of Songs in the Bible. Read lines such as these and tell me that religion isn't joyful:

> Let him kiss me with the kisses of his mouth—
> for your love is more delightful than wine.
> Pleasing is the fragrance of your perfumes;
> your name is like perfume poured out.
> No wonder the young women love you!
> Take me away with you—let us hurry!
> Let the king bring me into his chambers.
>
> —Song of Songs 3:2–4

If you have the wrong attitude, you can suck the life out of anything—religion, life, love, even sex. So if you're not benefiting from all the joy that life has to offer, don't make excuses, especially when it comes to religion. Instead, examine that which is causing you to stifle your emotions and find ways of turning matters around so that you're helped in living a rich life instead of hindered.

≈

I just mentioned that I am friends with several cantors. I am also very good friends with a conductor, Matthew Lazar, and the combination of these gentlemen—along with my longtime television producer, John Lollos—resulted in what I feel is a very entertaining and interesting film entitled *A Jewish Spirit Sings* that I appeared in and helped produce.

The inspiration for this video was my book, *Musically Speaking: A Life through Song (with Jerry Singerman, PhD)*. Many people felt that the story of the role that music played in my life, despite me being someone who doesn't sing, deserved an additional format. Maestro Lazar, whom I'll refer to as Mattie from now on, runs a New York City–based group, the Zamir Choral, and every year Mattie and his wife, Vivian, bring together those who sing in Jewish chorals from all across the country—over five hundred singers every year—to the North American Jewish Choral Festival. The amount of singing that takes place—whether in large groups rehearsing for the final performances, or in groups of twos and threes sitting on the lawn or strolling along the winding roads—is staggering. You don't have to understand the words to feel the magic that all these voices circulating freely through the countryside provide. In 2008, I was to get an award at that festival, and so it seemed a great opportunity to produce a film that would bring all these elements together. The result was *A Jewish Spirit Sings*.

There were many highlights during the long weekend we spent at the Hudson Valley Resort and Spa in the Catskills, but my favorite moments were those that brought together my three favorite cantors: Joseph Malovany (Fifth Avenue Synagogue), Alberto Mizrahi (Anshe Emet Synagogue, Chicago), and Jacob Mendelson (Temple Israel Center in White Plains, New York, retired). When you listen to one of these fantastic cantors singing in a synagogue, the performance is a key part of the liturgy and hence a very serious and dignified part of the service. But up in the Catskills, the three great singers were given a chance to let their true personalities shine through. Cantor Mendelson calls himself a humorist, and in fact he can be extremely funny even while singing religious music. A duet he performed with Cantor Mizrahi of *"Chad Gadya"* (which is the last song sung at a Passover seder), backed up by the Zamir Choral, had the entire audience smiling broadly as well as clapping and stomping their feet. Each man would sing a verse and then the other would repeat it, but in a fun, energetic way, a sort of "Can you top this" that you would never see two cantors do normally. It was this combination of the religious music—the distinguished cantors and the joy that was emanating from that stage as the two men competed—that made it an unforgettable moment for me as well as the audience, which cheered loudly after the number ended.

I don't know much about popular music, but the problem with it, as I see it, is that it has shallow roots. When each generation listens to different music instead of music that keeps a culture and society together, it can end up dividing us. (And when people are listening via headphones so that they are separated from the world . . . don't get me started!) There can be so much power in music, but that power is felt at its strongest when it binds an entire people together—sort of what happens when we sing the national anthem at a ball game. That's not to say that there's anything wrong with pop music. As a society, though, we shouldn't allow it to completely overshadow the rest of our musical heritage. Let me give you two examples of the important role that music played in my life, both similar, as they occurred on long train rides, and yet both so different.

On that long ago train to Switzerland, the tears were flowing on almost every face. And how could they not? We were physically whole, but emotionally we'd been torn apart from that which mattered most to us, our families. I'd done what I could for that little girl by giving up my favorite doll, but I was left miserable and had no way of pulling myself together when everywhere I looked, all I could see on the faces around me was even more misery. So despite my lack of talent, I started singing. And whether it was to join my voice or drown me out, all the other children began singing too. We sang for ten hours straight—all the songs we'd learned from our families—until we reached our destination. We didn't just sing those songs; we clung to them. They were our life raft as we drifted away into an unknown ocean. Just as Moses led the Israelites in song to give them courage as they crossed the Red Sea, we all took courage in the songs from our childhood. Never mind that many were of German origin rather than Jewish. We were children and didn't understand the politics of Nazi Germany. These were the songs our parents had sung to us and that we'd sung during the holidays; the notes wrapped around us as if we somehow were still in the arms of our parents. And to this day, when I go to synagogue and hear "Tzadik Katamar," which I used to listen to seated next to my father on Friday nights, I can almost feel his hand on mine.

On the next important train ride of my life, as we left Switzerland for Toulon, France, where we would board the ship for Palestine, all of us sang for most of the journey. Again, we were going off to a strange land, but our singing wasn't an effort to cover our fear; it was an expression of the hope and joy we felt at heading toward a land that we so urgently wished would become the home we didn't have. And again, these songs were mostly in German. What we didn't know then was that when we arrived in Palestine, they'd mostly disappear from the repertoire of what we sang aloud. Most of the Jews already in Palestine were from other lands, many from Poland, and they didn't want to hear anything German, as it reminded them of what the Germans had done to them. But at the time we sang them with gusto, lifting our voices to help us lift our spirits as our journey to the Promised Land began.

Of course, I never forgot those songs from my childhood. I have only a handful of pictures from those early years in Frankfurt, but what I have a bounty of, inside my head, are the songs that I heard over and over again in those happy moments. When I sing them to myself, it helps me to go back in time and relive those years when all was right with the world. You can't imagine how much comfort those songs have given me over my lifetime.

Jewish New York

I know there are some Jews who survived the Holocaust who gave up on their religion. They lost hope in God, and I certainly can't blame them for having that attitude. But rather than turn away from my religion, I turned toward it for comfort. I'd lost my family, so how could I throw away the traditions that they taught me? And the most important was being Jewish.

When I came to New York, I moved to Washington Heights, a neighborhood filled with German Jews, most of whom had escaped before the Nazis came to power and the door was slammed closed. In Washington Heights, I might still have people look down at me because of my height but not because of my background. I'd been forced into the life of a vagabond, but I didn't want to feel like a stranger the rest of my life, and in Washington Heights being a German Jew was the norm. If I didn't want to practice my broken English, I could walk into almost any shop and speak German. The delis stocked everything in terms of what I might consider comfort food. The newsstands carried German-language publications that I could read. In other words, I'd found a home. That was more than fifty years ago, and I'm still there—though the neighborhood has changed and there are fewer and fewer of us German Jews as it becomes a bit more posh. They've even started calling it "Hudson Heights," to differentiate it from the Washington Heights of lower down the hill that is mostly Dominican.

One of the centers of cultural life was and continues to be the YMHA of Washington Heights and Inwood. My husband, Fred, and I were members, and my two children spent many hours there. I was elected to the board and eventually was elected president, an office that I ended up holding for eleven years. And I'm proud to say that as president I never missed a meeting, though to be honest I did have to move some around so that I could maintain my perfect attendance record.

If you read the last paragraph quickly, you may not have paid much attention to those four initials, YMHA. Most people see that and think Young Men's Christian Association, but in this case and throughout New York City, many Y's substitute "Hebrew" for "Christian," as they are Jewish organizations. Nicknamed "schul with a pool," they serve to bind young Jews together. Individual temples may have a particular cohesion, either in their form (Judaism, Orthodox, Conservative, or Reform), or the background of their congregation (such as the German Jews of Washington Heights). But the Y could serve as a community center where all Jews could work together. And it was that aspect that drew my late husband and me to our Y.

To paraphrase what I said earlier, I never went Hollywood. I never even moved to Midtown Manhattan. But being a celebrity and living in Washington Heights has at times caused some clashes with my two lives, though as far as I'm concerned, so be it. For my seventy-fifth birthday bash, we decided to hold it at my Y. Most Y's aren't fancy establishments. They have a bit of a school-gym atmosphere, and my Y is no different. Where I live is very nice and safe. But lower Washington Heights is the type of neighborhood that many people shy away from, and though it's improved, they're not entirely wrong to do so. So luring some fancy people up to my Y took some doing. It didn't help that it poured that night, buckets and buckets, so that cabs were hard to find.

But I never let little things like a flooded kitchen bother me. (Yes, it rained so much that the Y's kitchen flooded.) I always do my best to have a good time, so while the guests were still coming in the main entrance dripping wet, I was off in the room where the band was playing, dancing with my good friend Malcolm Thomson. I may not be able to warble well, but I can cut the rug, as they say, and Malcolm and I were really swinging when Pierre came up to me with his cell phone held out and screamed, over the music, "You have a phone call."

I'm in the middle of a dance at my seventy-fifth birthday party and he expects me to take a phone call? Was it some press person wanting a quote? It could wait. I shooed Pierre away. But rather than listen, he kept waving me toward the exit. I circled the room in Malcolm's arms, but Pierre was still there as Malcolm and I came around—and he cut in in order to get me to stop dancing. I was furious, ready to blow the proverbial gasket. Then Pierre said, "It's President Clinton." Clinton was no longer president, but he was a favorite of mine. His offices were on 125th Street up in Harlem—not that far from where we were and Pierre had been working hard to get him to drop in—and for a while it looked as if he would, but as a next-best-thing he'd called to wish me a happy birthday. For that call it was worth suffering some dansus interruptus!

Mayor Dinkins did make it and spoke eloquently, and Arnold Schwarzenegger sent a bouquet of balloons. My rabbi sang in French, the Yale cellist Inbal Megiddo played beautifully, and somehow the Y's executive director and my very good friend, Marty Englisher, managed to get a meal served despite the rising water in the kitchen.

One of the great benefits of surrounding yourself with joie de vivre is that you tend to attract people to your side. People want to be around you because they get to share in some of your positive energy. You don't have to become best friends with all of them, but having a circle of friends who support you is worth having. And one benefit of making yourself the life of the party is that wherever you go, a party seems to appear!

～

You may have noticed I called the Washington Heights Y "my Y." Additionally I call the Museum of Jewish Heritage—A Living Memorial to the Holocaust, "my" museum, as I sit on the board. Most of the other board members have given huge amounts of money, so would be in a better position to call it their museum, but as I'm the only board member who is actually an orphan of the Holocaust, I say I get to claim it.

I am very proud to sit on this board, and the reason is quite sad. Nobody has to like anyone else, and if some people want to hate the Jews, for whatever reason, that's their business. But no matter what you think of us, facts are facts: the Holocaust happened and six million Jews were murdered, my family members among them. Holocaust deniers are truly despicable people, spreading their lies when real people who suffered and died deserve to be honored, not slandered. I suppose the deniers think that all Jews do nothing but try to get ahead based on the fact that we were almost annihilated. All the Nobel prizes and other awards that Jews around the world have won were given out of sympathy? That Israel is thriving while the countries around it are languishing simply because the world feels sorry for Jews? This is nonsense. But if lies get told enough times, people believe them, and so we need institutions like my museum to counter those lies with the truth.

Jews are not perfect. Nobody is perfect but God. There are bad people of every religion, as well as among atheists, and there are good ones. But it seems that Jews are always having to prove to the rest of the world that we're not bad. And so to play a role in an institution such as the Museum of Jewish Heritage is a continuation of the fight I joined when I became a member of the Haganah. Every time I generate some media attention for the museum that brings more people through the door, it's as if I'd fired those bullets into a bull's-eye, and that makes me very happy.

What doesn't make me happy is that our board meetings are held early in the morning. I normally don't get up until 9:00 a.m., and so to be all the way down at Battery Park by 8:30 is a sacrifice, though where we meet is gorgeous. The museum sits at the end of Manhattan on the Hudson River. The architects did a terrific job (in more ways than just the beauty of the design, as none of the rising waters caused by Hurricane Sandy breached the building's defenses.) Our boardroom is on the top floor, and it has glass walls in a V shape so that you look out on the Statue of Liberty, Ellis Island, and all of

New York Harbor. I have to confess that when the meeting turns to the nitty-gritty details, my attention is often more focused on the boats going to and fro than the budgetary numbers being thrown at us. I rely on my friends on the board—especially attorney Jeff Tabak, who reads every word—to guide me when it comes time to vote.

When I first joined the board, there was an exhibition that meant a lot to me. It featured Jewish soldiers in the American Army during World War II. And among the photos on the wall was one of my Fred Westheimer (and here I can truly use the word "my"!). Fred was a German Jew like me, but his family had escaped to Portugal in 1938—they were smart enough to see what was coming. Then Freddy came to the States, where he joined the US Army to fight Hitler. It made me proud to see Freddy's photo on the walls of the museum, and I was sad when the exhibit was changed. By that point, Fred had passed away, and whenever I went there, I had made sure to visit him.

I think it's worth repeating here that feelings of sadness—and I felt sad when I went to look at Fred's photo as a handsome soldier—are a part of joie de vivre. Feeling the full range of emotions is a part of life. No one likes to feel sad, but assuming you're not clinically depressed, feeling sad from time to time is better than not feeling any emotions at all. And if you stifle your sadness, there's a good chance that you'll feel another emotion, guilt. Better to remember that person you lost for a few moments, be a little down and perhaps even cry a bit, but then shake those feelings off and the next time there's cause for celebration, be able to engage guilt-free.

≈

Jews are "known" for not having sex. That's a myth put out there by Jewish comedians who have discovered that they can get an easy laugh by complaining that their wives always seems to get headaches when the subject of sex is brought up. But the Jewish religion is very specific about the importance of sex. Not only is it a religious duty for a husband and wife to engage in sexual relations, but he must make sure that she is pleased—that is to say, has an orgasm. I wrote a whole book on this subject, *Heavenly Sex: Sex in the Jewish Tradition* (with Jonathan Mark of *Jewish Week*), so I'm not going to repeat myself here.

But despite being Jewish, despite having lost my family to the Nazis and having fought for Israel's independence, in the course of my career as Dr. Ruth, the only time I ran into protests about what I do was from my fellow Jews. It was 1982, and my radio show was just starting to take off. I was invited to give a lecture at a Jewish center in Rego Park, Queens, a place not thought of as a hotbed of conservatism. But it seems a small group of Orthodox thought that my appearing in this Jewish center was somehow offensive, and they made threats that they were going to demonstrate. If that were to happen today, I would just have canceled. Who needs that sort of aggravation? But back then, I didn't want to allow anyone to force me to back down from what I believed in. I knew that what I planned to say that evening was not anything shocking but actually a part of Torah, what the Jewish law says to do. It was the middle of June, and the week before I'd been out in LA to do *The Tonight Show* with Johnny Carson. Perhaps that type of national attention was what drew the protestors; I don't know. What I do know was that on the way out there, I was nervous. I'd had a talk with the director earlier that day.

"Dr. Ruth, I don't want to make you worried, but we've been told there are going to be demonstrators tonight."

For someone who'd been through Kristallnacht, the idea of demonstrators was actually a bit terrifying, even if I was told they were fellow Jews.

"Are you sure you can guarantee my safety?" I demanded.

"Yes, yes, I've been in touch with the local police captain, and he said that he'll maintain control."

Back in Germany, the police had looked on while ruffians beat up on Jews, and then they'd walked away. But I had a good relationship with the police department in New York. Every year my Y threw a breakfast for the local police precinct, and after I'd become famous, all the cops at the breakfast wanted my autograph so that they could show their wives. So part of me felt confident that I'd make it through the evening unscathed, and part of me felt very nervous, especially if this demonstration drew a lot of press coverage. A car was sent to get me. I sat very quietly in the back, which is not my style; normally I ask the driver all about himself. But on this evening I preferred to keep silent. I needed to gather myself so that when we arrived, if conditions were really out of control, I would have either the courage to be able to push through the demonstrators or the guts to say enough is enough and order the driver to turn around and get me home.

As we approached the Jewish center, I could see the police presence. There were at least fifty policemen in front of the building—some in riot gear—and there were a dozen police cars parked this way and that, blocking traffic. What I couldn't see were the demonstrators. We pulled up to the entrance; a big, burly policeman opened the door for me; and as I got out of the car, I could hear some shouting. Altogether there were eight demonstrators, who'd been penned behind some police barriers across the street. I couldn't hear what they were saying, and I didn't try to pick out their words as I walked quickly through the doors. I was relieved that the demonstration was minor, and very grateful for the show of support by the NYPD. And so in all these years of giving hundreds of lectures all around the world, that is really the only time that I was heckled in any way—and it was at the hands of my fellow Jews. Oy!

What was unfair about having those demonstrators at that event is that I am always so careful not to offend the Jewish community. When I speak to a Jewish group, I know that what I am saying is 100 percent appropriate for adults. (I never allow anyone under eighteen at my lectures when speaking to adults because I want to be able to give the audience permission to have good sex, a permission I wouldn't grant teens. At the same time, I also don't let adults in to my lectures when I am speaking to teens, as I know that it will make the teens feel uncomfortable and be less open to me. Both positions sometimes get some pushback, but I always stick to my guns.) For example, if I am asked to address a group on a Friday night and suspect that many in the potential audience might be Jews, I won't accept the date. I don't do this because of my religious objections to working on a Friday night but because it would exclude those Jews who wouldn't go to the event, and that would be insulting to them on my part.

Another example is the time I was asked to decorate a Christmas tree for a charity fund-raiser. Various celebrities were decorating trees near the holidays that would be auctioned off to raise money for the charity. It's something I wanted to do, but I wasn't going to decorate a Christmas tree. I came up with a compromise. Instead of calling my tree a Christmas tree, we called it a Hanukkah bush—I used little dreidels and other Jewish symbols in the decorating process. And the big winner was the charity, because a gentleman who became a friend of mine, David Mitchell, bid $10,000 for my tree, and then he bid an additional $10,000 so that another had to be made. Wow.

By the way, just because I wouldn't decorate a Christmas tree doesn't mean that I don't get along with Christians, including members of the Catholic clergy. I was once dining at the Four Seasons restaurant when I noticed that there was a group dining in a private dining area. I didn't know who was in that room, but I'm not shy and I'm always curious, so I peeked inside. It was all priests and nuns, and they greeted me with enthusiasm and insisted I come in to say hello to them all. And despite my stand in favor of the right to abortion, even New York's Cardinal Dolan seems to be a fan. Before the Steuben Parade (the German American parade I was made grand marshal of, which I mentioned earlier), Mass was celebrated in St. Patrick's Cathedral. Of course I attended and was seated in the first row, both because I was an honored guest and also because I always make sure I'm in the first row so that I can see what's going on. After the cardinal said the Mass, he came over to greet all the dignitaries. When he came to me, he gave me a big smile and a kiss on the cheek while I put my hand on his cheek. So this little Jew gets around!

I mentioned earlier that Jews are actually instructed to have satisfying sex—that is to say, sex where both partners reach orgasm. This certainly applies to Orthodox Jews, who must also obey other religious strictures, including one not to engage in sexual relations while the wife is having her period and for seven days after that. At that point she goes to the *mikvah*, a ritual bath. When she comes home, the couple can have sexual relations. Here's one more case where you could look at the glass being half empty or half full. You could say that because of their religion, almost half of the time Orthodox Jews are not allowed to have sex. Or else you could say that every month, after this time set aside for abstinence, they are literally desperate to get into bed with each other, and that those times when they have sex are the best times because of their heightened arousal. Joie de vivre is a matter of attitude, and anyone who takes a positive attitude toward sex can actually find great pleasure, no matter what the challenges.

I know that the readers of this book aren't necessarily Jewish and may not even believe in God. Most anyone can experience joie de vivre; however, those who are cynical to the extreme and believe in nothing will have a much harder time. Being a human is very special. You don't have to believe that God has given us our life force, but if you look at the world without appreciating all the blessings we have, the beauty of the earth, the goodness and kindness of its inhabitants, the love that can be shared, then you'll never feel real joy. So . . . believe in *something* and embrace your passions!

CHAPTER IV

Open Yourself Up to Love: My History in Love and Marriage

What is life without love? And what is love without heartache? I've had three husbands. In two cases, it's the love that died; in the third—and longest—it was my husband who passed away. But as Edith Piaf sang, "*Je ne regrette rien.*" I don't regret any of it because without the vibrancy of love, life is very pale.

A lot of young people go through an awkward stage, but eventually they grow out of it, and soon enough someone from the opposite sex is showing some interest in them. Since I'm only four foot seven, I never entirely grew out of my awkward stage, and for a long time in my youth I was certain that no man would ever find me attractive. I've already told you about my first boyfriend, Putz, and the male nurse with whom I had an affair—and that I've had three husbands—so obviously, my predictive powers were off back then. But I also know that my realistic assessment of my situation was important because it helped me to be proactive. If I couldn't rely on my statuesque figure to lure men, then I had to have a backup plan. And part of that was exhibiting joie de vivre, even though at that time I had no idea what that meant. On the one hand, I felt very low when I was by myself, very unsettled with my life in Palestine, and even more uncertain about my future. On the other hand, when I was with my friends—say, at the dances that we had on the kibbutz on Friday nights—I let my real personality shine through, and the male friends that I'd made responded appropriately. Of course I did more than just be myself. For example, there was one man I liked and who liked me. Actually, he liked me more than I liked him, but I certainly liked the attention. I figured out how to time it so that when he went to lunch at the kibbutz, I'd go in at exactly the same time and we'd sit together. This technique had the desired effect, and his affection for me grew. However, when I met his brother (who was a soldier—I found his uniform very sexy), I quickly changed my sights, and future sniper that I would become, I hit the mark.

But during all of this, there was another man who was my real object of desire. We were friends, and the time we'd spend together was both satisfying and frustrating: he liked someone else "that way." Unrequited love is a joie de vivre killer because your heart is stuck on someone who doesn't feel the same way about you. Every time you're with that person, you're walking on air, your hopes soaring with the slightest glance or casual touch. But then, as soon as you're apart, you're faced with the reality of your situation, that this person is really unavailable to you. I get questions from people caught in such situations, and my advice to them is to keep yourself as far from this person as possible. That might mean switching schools, jobs, or even cities. To feel joie de vivre to its fullest, you can't have this glass ceiling above you that keeps you from soaring.

I lost my virginity on the kibbutz. I won't say with whom because I am still friendly with him and he is married to someone else—and she and I are friends too—but it was in a hayloft, which provided not only privacy but a softer environment than our hard beds, and it was wonderful. We visited that hayloft again and again (and that I didn't wind up pregnant was a minor miracle, because we weren't using any form of birth control).

One phrase that the French use for an orgasm is *la petite mort*, "the little death." It's meant to describe not so much the orgasm itself as that feeling you get right afterward, a slight blackout one might feel, as the life forces you exerted leave your body for a while. And, in fact, if an orgasm is strong enough, you might feel like you're going to burst open and die. In that sense, one could almost say that an orgasm goes beyond joie de vivre—you experience death in some small way, rather than life. But that's not true, because actually joie de vivre encompasses many more emotions than only joy.

To fully live life, there's an entire range of emotions that you need to feel, and that even includes sadness. If you experience only happy times, you're going to appreciate them less than if you can compare them to sad times. So a feeling such as nostalgia isn't exactly joyful, but it's an emotional experience that makes you more alive. Joie de vivre isn't only about experiencing joy, but being open to all your feelings.

Let me illustrate with a personal example, one of motherly love. My daughter Miriam went to Israel and served in the Israeli Defense Forces. Of course, I missed my daughter because she wasn't nearby. And I worried about her because being in the army, even if there is no war, is inherently dangerous, as there are firearms and training exercises. But I was also very proud of her for showing the same devotion to Israel that I had. As an American, she didn't have to go to join the army. But it was something that as a Jew she felt was important. And then when she moved back to New York, the elation I felt at having her back was indescribable! While she was away, my heart hurt, but I would call her as often as possible, visit when I could, and pray that she would come home safely. I didn't let her being over there kill my joie de vivre, because having a child leave home is part of life. But boy, was I excited at having her back!

I could have gone around with a long face the entire time Miriam was in Israel. But working yourself up over something that you can't change is a mistake. It's OK to spend a few minutes every day being sad or worrying, but then you have to put those negative emotions aside, because life is too precious to waste even one day of it.

~

I met my first husband through the surgeon who had tended to my legs after the bomb blast in 1948. David was a soldier in the Israeli army, and as I've told you, I seem to favor men in uniforms. He was also from a comparatively wealthy family in Tel Aviv and planned on being a doctor. I was surprised that he fell in love with me because I still thought of myself as unattractive and short, though luckily David was short as well, so that gave me an advantage over all the taller girls.

If I was surprised at David's proposal of marriage, his father was disappointed. He thought we were too young, and that David could have done better than a refugee. But we got married anyway and moved to Paris. David was out of the army by then, and since there was no medical school in Israel, we set off to the City of Lights.

I've been throwing a variety of French phrases at you, and it was in Paris where I learned them all. But living in Paris meant that I learned not only their meaning as you would in a dictionary, but I learned what they meant as I lived in this magical city. If you've spent a few days in Paris seeing all the famous sites surrounded by tourists, then you've missed the real city and its magic. When David and I were there, we were really poor. Our apartment was an unheated, furnished room on the third floor of a walk-up with cold water and no bathroom. The toilet—if you want to call a stand-up "Turkish" variety a toilet—was two floors down. And yet I loved every second in Paris.

Most of my friends were fellow Israeli students living on next to no money. (And our financial situations actually worsened while we were there; Israel imposed currency limitations, and David's parents couldn't send us the funds they'd been directing to David's expenses. I was teaching in a Jewish kindergarten but was paid very little.) When we went to a café, we'd share one cup of coffee. We could window-shop, *faire du lèche-carreau* (literally, "lick the shop windows") but not buy anything. But it was still possible, with student discounts, to eat decently, see the occasional movie, and go to La Comédie-Française to watch a show. And even if you were far down the rungs of the economic ladder, living in Paris meant that you were still part of it all, a Parisian. That thought still makes my heart jump a little.

David and I both learned as much French as we could because the French are very proud of their language, and if you wanted to fit in and make French friends, you had to speak their language. We were able to enjoy so much more of what Paris had to offer, even if we couldn't afford the luxury items which surrounded us.

After having spent so many years being very poor, I certainly appreciate the importance of money. But while money can be of assistance in enjoying life, especially when it comes to making sure you have the necessities, you can most certainly generate joie de vivre in many ways that don't cost a penny. As I've mentioned, during the holidays I head to Fifth Avenue to look at the window displays, and I go to parades and look out my window to watch the sunset. What's vital is to have the right attitude. Any one of these experiences can create a glow that lasts for hours. A walk, be it on city streets looking at the people around you or in a park absorbing Mother Nature, can be very uplifting, but you have to force yourself to get out and *take* that walk with the idea that you're going to absorb joie de vivre with every step.

This recollection of Paris reminds me of one of my later trips there. It was 1985, my television show on Lifetime was doing great, I'd been on the covers of *People* and *TV Guide*, I was giving lectures all over the country, writing books—to say my plate was full was no exaggeration. And in the middle of all this comes an invitation to be in a movie that was being shot in France. Given how busy I was, that I agreed to do it wasn't so much taking a risk as it was an act of insanity. But while I loved the years I'd spent in France, I'd been poor as a church mouse, huddling in cafes for hours over one cup of coffee. And so the chance for me, who had spent so many evenings in the last row of the balcony at La Comédie-Française, to go back to be a French movie star was just too tempting to pass up.

The director was Daniel Vigne, best known for his award-winning film *The Return of Martin Guerre*. He'd had Linda Hunt in mind for the role of Mrs. Heffner, as being short was a critical aspect, but she hadn't agreed to it yet, so he flew to New York to interview me. We met at a Midtown hotel. I went mostly out of curiosity, but before I met Daniel, someone downstairs in the lobby told me that he'd already chosen Linda Hunt. That got my competitive spirit going. Since I was still going to read for the role, I decided to give it my best shot. Daniel is a real charmer, and since you know my second husband was French, you can understand that I have a thing for handsome Frenchmen. But whatever it was that afternoon (and in all probability, whoever said that Linda Hunt had been chosen didn't know what they were talking about), I gave it my all, and Daniel said to me, "You're hired."

The film was a romantic comedy with one of those convoluted plots the French are known for and if you can believe it, it involved the six-foot-tall Sigourney Weaver being mistaken for the four-foot-seven me. But if the plot was convoluted, it was no more so than my life had become. Now I had to somehow integrate flying to Paris for five or six days at a time into a schedule that already left me no time to breathe. I had Pierre cancel some lectures (so not only did this role not pay me very much, but it cost me some money), but I still had a TV show to do. And the live shows couldn't be taped, so I had to be there, and alive, or at least awake. No one knew except my producer, John Lollos, my cohost, Larry Angelo, and some of the crew; but on one of these late nights when I'd just returned from Paris, I actually nodded off at the end of the show. John spotted it and told the stage manager to signal to Larry; they kept the camera on him while the stage manager came over and tapped me on the shoulder. Luckily I'm used to taking catnaps. I was able to quickly pick up the reins, and even such a short breather gave me an energy boost.

In the movie, actor Gérard Depardieu plays an anthropologist who goes to the airport a day early to meet a philanthropist (me) and instead winds up picking up Sigourney. On one day of filming, I was outside the apartment building in which we were to shoot a scene, waiting for them to tell me to go upstairs. I walked over to the building next door and tried the door, but it was locked. I stood there looking up at the building when Michel Aumont, another terrific actor in the film, came over to me.

"Docteur Ruth, we are filming in that building, not this one."

"Michel," I answered, "I know, but I wanted to see if I could get a glimpse inside of this one."

"*Mais pourquoi?*" (Because I lived in France for five years, my French is pretty good, and this conversation actually was in French.)

"When I first came to France, this is where I lived. On the top floor," I said, pointing up. "Every day I had to walk up and down all those stairs. And with my short legs, that wasn't easy. There was no heat in the building. Or hot water. And the toilet was two stories below."

"And now here you are, starring in a French movie, being filmed right next door. I can understand why you look so contemplative."

"When I lived here, my goal in life was to be a kindergarten teacher. I didn't have stars in my eyes but was very down-to-earth. To be right back here in this very same spot, so many years later, making a movie, it's all very hard to process."

"You still see yourself as that young woman."

"Of course, and if I could go back in time and describe what is happening here today to the me of back then, she would have had a good laugh and told me to be on my way. It's almost as if there are two of me here. The young me, struggling to get by, and the Dr. Ruth me, acting in a movie one building over."

A production assistant came up and asked us to follow him inside the building where we were filming, but I didn't move right away. I was still lost in thought. How could *that* Ruth have become *this* Ruth? How could *that* Ruth have wound up making a movie with one of France's greatest actors, being directed by one of France's best directors, alongside one of America's most famous actresses? It was such an amazing experience that I had to walk away because if I'd let myself dwell on it any longer, I would never have been able to say my lines.

On the next trip over to France, we did a scene in the Salle Richelieu in the Sorbonne. I had flunked an exam in physiology in the very same room! Again as I looked around I couldn't help but psychologically pinch myself because this journey I'd made was so unbelievable. Then a big smile came to my face as I thought, "If only my classmates and teacher from back then could see me now!"

And that's why to come back to Paris to star in a film was so moving. Had that movie been made anywhere else in the world, I might not have agreed to disrupt my life to be in it. In fact, I have turned down other movie roles, though mostly because the producers didn't want me to play a part but just be Dr. Ruth (a famous movie critic once told me never to do that, and I listened). But this film was to be shot in Paris, where I had once felt so poor; to live the life of a movie star, even for only a few weeks, was an offer that was just too tempting.

And that scene in the Sorbonne? It ended in a food fight! How much fun was that!

In the movie, Gérard Depardieu falls for the imposter, so my character doesn't give him any money. But in real life he was a generous man who threw a party for the cast in a wine cellar alongside the Seine. Everybody had a wonderful time drinking a lot of wine, especially Gérard. Even though I didn't have more than a sip, I couldn't have been flying any higher.

And while I'm on Paris experiences, here's one more—a chance that I took that has a French beret sort of ending. I was approached to do a book on art. I'm always going to museums, but it's not that all those visits have made me an art expert. However, the publisher, Abbeville, paired me with a curator from the Metropolitan Museum of Art, Gary Tinterow (now the director of Houston's Museum of Fine Arts), and the deal was that he would supply the expertise in his field and I'd do the same in mine. The book, still in print, is titled *The Art of Arousal*, and I'm very proud of it. I think it's a good book for couples to share because while the art has plenty of erotic content, it's far from pornographic—it's a book that a husband and wife can share without anyone getting offended, and perhaps both partners will become just a little bit aroused.

As satisfied as I was with that book, when it came out in French, I was even more delighted, especially because the French edition was in a fancy boxed cover. And then Gary and I were invited to do a signing at the Louvre! I'd spent hours and hours in the Louvre when I lived in Paris, and to have a book that I'd written sold there pleased me to no end. French movies are one art form, but the movie I was in wasn't of the serious type, so to have my book sold in the Louvre meant a lot to me. Maybe I wouldn't be hanging next to the Mona Lisa, but at least I was sharing the same building with her!

At one point while Gary and I were walking in Paris, I spotted a coat in the window of a fancy dress shop. It was red with a black velvet collar. I normally don't lust after clothes, but I fell in love with that coat right away, *le coup de foudre*, as the French would say. I dragged Gary inside but sadly they didn't have one in my size. However they said they were willing to make one and while the price was *très cher*, I said yes. Gary was going back to Paris in a month, and he volunteered to pick it up for me. I wore that coat for years and was really sad when it became too threadbare to keep.

What especially distinguished the extravagance of this coat when compared to my usual spending budget is that when I travel, my norm is to pick up a lot of trinkets to give as presents. Some I keep for myself, but most of them I give when I need to thank someone. When in Paris, one place I always stop is a gift shop on the Rue de Rivoli, the covered street opposite the Tuileries. At this shop where you have to go down a few steps to enter, I always stock up on little Limoges items, especially the little plates. I know they're kitschy, but I like them. (I have a friend for whom I'm always picking up golf balls when I travel. The last time he went to Paris he got me a Limoges golf ball!)

When I was just turning ten, I never would have imagined that our family was soon to be broken up. On my twentieth birthday, I never thought that I'd be caught in a bomb blast. And when I was studying in Paris, in my wildest dreams I would never have come back to star in a movie. You know every day I read my horoscope in the *New York Post* because it's entertaining, but if there's anyone who recognizes that you can't predict the future, it's me. These are surprises on a grand scale, but every day you will find yourself caught off guard by something. Some will be good and some might not be so good but surprises are part of life. Trying to protect yourself from shocks or changes is similar to trying to tamp down emotions such as sadness; you may end up more dead than alive. Instead you must learn to embrace surprises. Obviously if you or a loved one are given a terrible medical diagnosis, that's not something you can feel good about, but it's also an experience you can't prevent either. So make sure that when a good surprise comes along, you enjoy it fully so that when the bad one inevitably hits, at least it won't have ruined all the good ones. Imagine a man never having sex with a partner because he was afraid that one time he might not be able to have an erection. People follow such lines of logic and wind up living poorer lives because of it. Don't fall prey to such behavior.

～

Ah, but back to my story and to my initial years in France. My first husband, David, was in medical school, and just about every one of our friends was a student. I was teaching kindergarten but without even a high school diploma, and any chance to get a college degree that would further my original goal of being a doctor—of some sort, anyway—was out of the question. But then the French government, realizing that the war had played havoc with the educational path of so many young people, created a way of entering the Sorbonne. They offered a one-year course, and anyone who could pass it could then enroll into the main student body. I signed up and a year later was able to enter the Institute of Psychology at the Sorbonne, working toward a *license*, which was somewhere between a bachelor's and a master's degree. It was going to be quite a difficult undertaking given my skills in French, but talk about joie de vivre! I was walking on air.

And for my classes, I was often up in the air. Classes at the Sorbonne are given in large amphitheaters; due to my schedule, I was never able to get there early enough to get a seat. My solution was to ask a taller male student to lift me up and place me on a window ledge, so I ended up having the best seat in the house!

I know that many people in that situation would never have the nerve to ask for such help or put themselves on display like that. They'd just stand in the back, not being able to see anything. But obtaining joie de vivre takes some courage. I'm short, so I always push myself toward the front. I see no reason why I should be held back by my height. Sometimes it's even an advantage, because people let me push through because of my size, and being in the front allows me to interact more than if I were somewhere in the middle. Plus, once you push yourself forward a couple of times and see that it works, it makes it easier to do again and again. You gain experience and learn that even when it doesn't work, it's not the end of the world. But you can't hesitate when pushing yourself. You have to know that you're going to do it and just act. If you go back and forth in your mind, playing a game of "Should I or shouldn't I," you probably won't push yourself. You know the saying, "He who hesitates is lost"? Well, it's true. But once you get a taste for winning because you pushed a little harder, you won't hesitate because you won't want to put up with feeling less than a winner.

I was at Madison Square Garden when Bill Clinton accepted the Democratic nomination the first time he ran for president. Not only was I there, I was sitting right in front with the Arkansas delegation. I'd told Bill to run, so I was sharing fully in the excitement of the moment, not somewhere up in the balcony with the television network that had brought me there. That's how you grab the most intense sensations that life has to offer, by going after them, not waiting for them to miraculously land in your lap. Every once in a while the lottery might hit your lap, but more often than not it's those who go after what they want that get it.

As I said earlier, joie de vivre also includes some sadness, because if you're living in the real world, not everything is going to go perfectly. And so it was with my marriage to David. He'd decided that he didn't want to be a doctor and went back to Israel to get a master's in Middle Eastern studies. I went with him, but when the semester started again at the Sorbonne, I went back to Paris. Some long-distance relationships can work but ours wasn't meant to be. David's father had been right; we were too young. We eventually got a divorce, by mail.

If there's one lesson that life has taught me, it's to waste as little time as possible. No matter how long you live, the years go by so quickly that to waste even seconds is a pity. And that's why when a couple comes to my office and it's obvious that they're not right for each other, I tell them to separate as quickly as possible. Why waste more of your precious life being miserable when there's another way? Being able to cut one's losses is vital to experiencing the most joie de vivre. There's some misery that's unavoidable, such as having a terrible disease, but marriages can be dissolved and if that's going to be the ultimate decision, then it should be done quickly. I'm still friends with my former husbands—perhaps in part because we didn't stretch out our marriages to the point where they became painful, so there was very little bitterness.

I met my second husband, Dan, at a coffeehouse in Paris through some Israeli friends. He didn't have a career, but he was good-looking, kind, and sweet, and so we started a wonderful love affair. And then, even though I just told you not to expect anything to drop into your lap, a gift dropped into mine. I had not asked Germany for any reparations, but I was sent a check for $1,500 from the West German government to those who had suffered Nazi war crimes and not finished their education. While I hadn't asked for anything from Germany, I wasn't about to send such a sum of money back.

"Dan, look at what I received in the mail."

Dan looked at the check and whistled. "You were wondering how you were going to pay for the rest of your education. Now you know."

"I've been thinking about it, and I've come to the decision that since I intend to go back to Israel, what's the use of working so hard for this French degree?"

"But you've been telling me how important getting an education is. In fact, just the other day you were scolding me for not going back to take classes."

"You don't necessarily need to be in a school to get an education."

"Now you're sounding like me."

"And maybe you're a bad influence on me, but I've decided to use this money to go to America. I have an uncle in San Francisco whom I haven't seen since I was three years old, and some of my friends from Heiden are there, and I just feel drawn to visiting the United States."

"Really." Dan looked a little sad as he said this.

"Oh, I didn't tell you the best part. I want you to go with me!"

We bought fourth-class tickets on the *Liberté*. Even though we weren't supposed to be on deck, we snuck up and stayed up waiting all night to see the Statue of Liberty. We met some friends in New York and stayed in a hotel the first night but knew we couldn't afford that option for very long. I knew there was a German Jewish newspaper called the *Aufbau*, and I bought a copy, hoping to find a cheap room advertised. But what caught my eye was a large ad placed by the Graduate Faculty of Political and Social Science of the New School for Social Research announcing a scholarship open to Nazi victims seeking a master's degree in sociology. I went right down there, and within twenty-four hours, I had the scholarship. We also found a small room to rent in Washington Heights only four blocks from where I live today, which is not so surprising since Washington Heights was a German Jewish enclave.

Since the scholarship only paid for my tuition, we needed money to live on. Our landlady knew of someone looking for a housemaid. I may not have had any degrees, but I did have that certificate as a Swiss housekeeper. The couple that hired me—at the whopping price of seventy-five cents an hour—was from Frankfurt; she had even attended the same school I had. But my days as a maid wouldn't last long. Soon after, Dan found both of us jobs at the French embassy, and I got a 25 percent raise, to a dollar an hour.

I had trouble with the classes because of the language barrier, until in one class I discovered two German students who were taking notes in a language that I could actually comprehend. On the one hand, you could say that fate was smiling down on me, but if I hadn't turned around to ask for their help, I wouldn't have seen that smile. Life can be beautiful, but you have to be ready to grab those brass rings as the carousel swings you around and around.

Fate had another surprise in store for me: I was pregnant. For some reason I'd assumed that I couldn't get pregnant, maybe because I was so short. (I always talk to students about sexual myths, such as having hair grow on the palm of your hand from masturbating, but ironically I never mention this particular myth that snared me. Since my parents were both short, maybe they fell into the same trap!) Because of the coming baby, Dan and I decided to get married. I was in heaven despite the fact that I was throwing up every morning. To me, that nausea was absolutely an integral part of joie de vivre, both for me and my baby, and I never once complained. And the joy I felt when Miriam was born was unbelievable. I'd lost my entire family to the Nazis, but now I had started a new one of my own.

When Miriam was one year old, Dan and I separated. What we'd had was a great love affair, but there wasn't enough of a connection to sustain a marriage that would last a lifetime. One of the missing ingredients was intellectual stimulation. I often speak about sexual boredom, and it's certainly a topic that magazines like *Cosmo* address regularly, but in my opinion, sexual boredom is only a minor aspect to a couple's not having a satisfying sex life. Intellectual boredom with each other is a much bigger culprit.

There are some people who have developed a certain style of reaching orgasm that requires them to act in a certain way each and every time. Now, couples where one or both have this issue can use other positions and try out other ways to boost their sex life, but in the end they'll have to have sex using that one tried-and-true way in order to both end up sexually satisfied. So you might think that such a couple's relationship wouldn't be stable since their sex life is so predictable. But that wouldn't necessarily be true at all. If the rest of their life together is filled to the brim with intellectual stimulation—which could mean that they are constantly going to concerts and visiting museums and reading and discussing books, or simply sharing a hobby, like gardening, and spending hours poring over seed catalogs—then their relationship would be a strong one. And that strong relationship would spill over so that their sexual attraction for each other would also remain potent. On the other hand, a couple whose sex life resembles a porn movie but who, outside of the bedroom, bore each other to tears, just wouldn't last.

Here I've given you extremes, which was not the case for Dan and me. But young mother that I was, I was wise enough to see into our future, and I didn't see it being a fulfilling one. Even though it meant that I was going to have to raise Miriam by myself, or at least until I'd found someone else, I knew the right move was to divorce Dan, who went back to France and wasn't a part of Miriam's or my life anymore. I knew he had no money and was unlikely to have any soon, so I didn't expect or ask for support. In those days, the only possible form of communication was by letter, and frankly, between raising and supporting Miriam and going to school at night, I didn't have a free moment to put pen to paper, and I suppose neither did he. After a time I took Miriam to Mexico, where I obtained a divorce. Dan and I didn't entirely lose touch, though having the Atlantic Ocean between us didn't serve to strengthen our relationship any.

Was there sadness in our parting? Of course—but mostly for what might have been. I knew I'd be happier without Dan tagging along because the potential for the rest of my life had improved. And in that knowledge I found joie de vivre. I didn't know where I was heading but at least I wasn't stuck in a rut going nowhere. Was I worried about being a single mother? I'd had to take care of myself since the age of ten, so I was used to shouldering the responsibility of day-to-day existence. I'd never had very much in terms of financial resources, but I'd always managed to get by and so I was confident that I'd be able to support myself and Miriam, who was the joy of my life.

CHAPTER V

Going After What You Want in Life

Having walked firsthand in a single mother's shoes, I know how difficult it can be to balance life and work. I didn't have any family to help me raise Miriam—a grandmother or two to fall back on, or even a distant cousin—so I had to rely on friends when the need arose. And it's this experience that led me to speak out when the lead character on the TV show *Murphy Brown* became a single mom. On TV, she could make it look easy, and that might convince some single women that they could follow in Murphy's footsteps without significant consequences. While I never regretted a second of my years raising Miriam by myself, given the difficulties, it's important to me to try to discourage anyone else with the idea of charting the same course. And at the top of my own list was to find someone who could join with me in the raising of my family.

My favorite word in the English language is "done." I dislike having things that are not completed littering my mind. To fully enjoy life, it's better if you don't have an overflowing to-do list constantly rattling around in your brain. Of course, some items on your list are easily taken care of, such as doing the dishes, while others take more time. More important, you also have less control over certain items, and finding a husband certainly falls under that category. So on the one hand, you mustn't become obsessive about it—that will only remove all possibilities of having joy on a day-to-day basis. But you also can't just leave it to chance. So whatever may be preventing you from saying "Done" needs to be neither at the front of your brain or way in the back, but somewhere in the middle so that you have enough incentive to push toward obtaining your goal—but not so much that you're miserable until you do.

One important resource that got me through this period was my circle of friends. Even as a single mother, I wasn't one to sit at home. If there was a party, I took Miriam and put her on the bed amid all the coats to sleep while we danced and talked in the next room. One of my friends, Dale Ordes, once suggested a ski weekend. I got some other friends to watch Miriam and off I went. Another friend on the trip was a Dutchman who worked with me, named Hans. We went up the mountain together, but the lift was a T-bar—which works fine when you're similar in height, but Hans was over six feet tall, and the combination just wasn't successful. When we got to the top, I was introduced to the president of the ski club we had joined for the weekend, Manfred Westheimer. Fred was short, and since he wasn't wearing a wedding ring, I could tell he was single.

"Hans, you know how you say I talk too much at work and you can't get your work done?"

"*Ja*, it's true."

"As it turns out, we're also not a great fit on a T-bar."

"*Ja*, I noticed that. Either it is under your neck or my ankles."

"Exactly. So you won't mind if from now on I go on the lift with that short one over there, Manfred."

"Ruth, I think that is an excellent idea."

I put the time Manfred and I shared on the T-bar to good use, and not only did we spend the day together, but we kept talking until two in the morning. The next day I called a friend and said, "I found the guy I'm going to marry." The only problem was that there were two other women in our group with the same idea, plus they had a head start. In fact, one of them was the woman I was sharing a room with, and she told me to keep my hands off her man. If you haven't noticed by now, I have a bit of a competitive spirit in me, and so her words had the opposite effect. Had she just looked sad, I might have felt sorry for her; but once she issued a challenge, I was even more eager.

Fred was an engineer, meaning he had a steady, well-paying job, which was reason enough for every single Jewish woman he met to start plotting how to land him. But he was also good-looking, friendly, and a great talker—and he played the guitar and the harmonica. He had a habit of telling stupid jokes that I didn't understand, but in the beginning I laughed anyway.

If there's something that you want out of life, half measures won't do, especially if you know that someone else wants the same thing that you do. Let me give you an example. Fred had left his guitar in the apartment of my main competitor. The last thing I wanted was for that guitar to be an excuse for Fred to go back there. What was I to do? I called Dale.

"Dale, I need to buy a guitar. Where should I go?"

"Ruth, what do you need with a guitar? You don't play and I doubt you ever will."

"Fred left his guitar at that other woman's place."

"And . . ."

"And I'm going to buy him a new one so he doesn't go over there to pick it up."

"Ruth, that's crazy." This from a man who would risk life and limb to ski down the mountain like a madman so that he could get as many runs in as possible to fully amortize his lift ticket.

"You say it's crazy, I say it would be crazy to let Fred anywhere near this woman's apartment. Where should I meet you?"

The guitar cost twenty-eight dollars, which to me was a small fortune. I didn't look at it as spending money but rather as an investment. By buying Fred a new guitar, not only was I keeping him out of the clutches of that other woman, but since Fred didn't have a clue as to why I bought him the guitar, I also scored brownie points for my generosity.

There's that saying again, "He who hesitates is lost." I saw danger in Fred going to that apartment, and I made sure to head it off at the pass. I could have hoped for the best, and maybe nothing would have happened—Fred would have picked up his guitar and come back to me, and I'd be twenty-eight dollars richer. But now weigh those twenty-eight dollars against the opposite scenario, losing Fred to the competition. That was not an acceptable outcome, so I made up my mind and carried out my decision.

I sometimes feel sorry for men who have to ask a woman out on a date. Often they get rejected, and that's hard to accept. I can see a man who's been turned down several times becoming gun shy, hesitating to ask the next woman out and thus letting opportunity after opportunity slip through his fingers. You can't really enjoy life if you're always hesitant. You have to make decisions, and while some of them won't turn out as planned, at least you'll know who to blame—and when they turn out to be right, you won't have to share the credit!

∾

Fred and some of his German Jewish friends had "discovered" a lake community in upstate New York called Lake Oscawana. Because the lake was rimmed by hills, to them it had a European feel, and they loved it so much that they wouldn't speak about it, afraid that outsiders might come and ruin it for them. Fred had a share in a summer house there; my rival had a share in the same house. That wasn't acceptable. I couldn't join their group because they wouldn't accept children and I couldn't leave Miriam on weekends. Then I discovered that the summer cabin next door was for rent, but the amount was way above my limited budget. I started calling friends to let them know of this great opportunity, and soon enough I'd lured in enough people that I would be spending the summer at Lake Oscawana. Little did I know at the time that one day I'd be calling the lake Fred's mistress, as he seemed to love it almost as much as me! But my first foray up there was successful. I couldn't keep Fred all to myself, because he had paid for his meals in his cottage—that wasn't something he would give up. So while he slept in our cabin, he ate next door!

Fred popped the question during a hike in the Catskills. We were sitting on a rock, resting.

"Ruth, will you marry me?"

"Fred, you know I will."

"Fine, but I have two conditions."

"Uh-oh," I thought to myself. "They'd better have nothing to do with that other woman."

"First, we have to get married by December thirty-first. That way we can file our taxes jointly which will save us both a lot of money."

I should have guessed that a man who would sleep with me but not eat with me to save money would come up with such a condition. "Fine, Fred, but you have to help make the arrangements since it's all so soon."

"Of course. And then I don't want you to tell anyone for two days."

Now, that was a tough condition for me to accept. I could say yes, but I wasn't sure I could fulfill my end of the deal when it came to such important news! "Fred, why two days? Can't I even tell Miriam?"

"I want my parents to know first is the reason, and if you tell Miriam, she's never going to keep it to herself. So you have to promise."

I promised—and I even kept the promise—and on December 10, 1961, we were married at the Windermere Hotel on the Upper West Side of Manhattan. All our friends were there, but our honeymoon lasted only one night, as Fred had to fly to Kansas on business.

Six months after our wedding, I became pregnant with our son Joel. Miriam was six when Joel was born, but there wasn't any sibling rivalry, in part because she was so much older and in part because I showered her with gifts to make sure that she wouldn't be jealous. All in all, I think I did a good job of raising my two children. One proof is that they both followed in my footsteps and received doctorates in education. (Yes, the "Dr." in Dr. Ruth comes from my EdD, not an MD, as many people mistakenly think—though I repeat that I am not a medical doctor over and over.) But what is difficult for parents is to keep up with the times, both in the general sense and in the personal one.

Let me give you an example. When Miriam was a teen, she begged me to get her own phone.

"But all the kids have them," she said.

"Maybe I should have sent you to public school where all the kids wouldn't have so much."

"It doesn't cost that much."

"And how would you know?"

"How can I stay in touch with my friends?"

"You're with them all day long—isn't that enough? You have to talk to them all night long too?"

"We talk about schoolwork. If I could work together with them on the phone, I could get better grades."

"Miriam, I wasn't born yesterday. The only subject matter that will be in these vital communications will be about boys. And it's not like we don't have a phone."

"Which you're on all the time!"

We had these fights over and over, but I wouldn't give in. When I was growing up, the idea of a young person having a phone of her own was unheard of. I doubt that even that Rothschild girl had one. To me it would have been spoiling Miriam, plus it would have been a distraction from her schoolwork. But you know what? I was wrong. I did spend a lot of time on the phone, so our home phone wasn't really available to her. And to her generation, talking on the phone was a key aspect to socialization. Not that Miriam wasn't popular, but I now understand the problems not having her own phone caused. And look at all the fights we could have avoided.

Joie de vivre can't be selfish. If the people around you are miserable because of your actions, that's going to make it harder for you to enjoy your life too. Certainly there are times when parents have to be tough, but you also have to be able to bend. You can't automatically say, "What was good enough for me is good enough for my children"; the world you grew up in no longer exists. And even if the world your spouse lived in was similar to yours, it wasn't the same either. So you have to give those around you some space to live and grow on their own. Spouses should do some things together, but it's also fine for them to do some things by themselves—though when the changes that result are major, the acceptance rate may not exactly match it. Certainly, going from Ruth Westheimer to Dr. Ruth wasn't that easy on my family.

⁓

Before I was Dr. Ruth, our family would go to a restaurant like everyone else, anonymously. But at one point that was no longer possible, and it didn't sit well. We did get to go to fancier restaurants than we had before, but often the reason we were there—my celebrity—got in the way. One restaurant I would take our family to was the Sea Grill, which overlooks the skating rink at Rockefeller Center. The maître d' would greet us warmly, and we'd get a table right by the window so we could see the skaters gliding by. But then other customers would stop by, either just to say hi or ask for an autograph.

"Mom, why do you put up with these interruptions?" Miriam or Joel would ask.

"Because the reason you're sitting at this prime table is because people are aware of who I am, and with fame comes certain obligations."

"You think Frank Sinatra gives autographs?"

"I'm not Frank Sinatra, and I bet even he gives the occasional autograph. Miriam, I have to go to the bathroom—come with me?"

"Why do you need me to go with you?"

"Because if I go alone, I'll get stopped by women asking me questions and I'll never get back to the table."

When I was not with family members but people I worked with, they understood what it's like to be famous; they'd go out of their way to make life easy for me. Thankfully I never got so famous that I had to deal with mobs that might even be dangerous, but my fame did lead to some awkward moments between me and my family members. Because of the sometimes negative reactions on both parts—them at being inconvenienced by celebrity, me being frustrated by their lack of appreciation of how I needed to act—I often kept my family away from events that I was invited to just because I was Dr. Ruth.

But there were some notable exceptions, such as when *60 Minutes* did a profile on me. Diane Sawyer came to our apartment in Washington Heights to do the sit-down interview portion. Under normal circumstances, I would have told Fred to stay away, but Fred was such a big fan of Diane that I didn't have the heart. So there we were in my living room, sitting on our Danish couch with Diane across from us and two cameras trained on us. It's an interview of me, but who does Diane address first? Fred.

"Mr. Westheimer, tell me, what is your sex life like?"

"Diane, the shoemaker's children don't have any shoes."

I should have been furious, but you know what? That story became a staple of all my lectures because it gets a big laugh. I don't talk about my sex life, just the way I don't talk about the sex lives of my clients. I'm a big believer in privacy, especially when it comes to sex. But a story like this one allows me to deflect the issue without seeming like I have anything to hide.

On the other hand, when I was invited to attend a party in the Playboy Mansion, I didn't have the heart to tell Freddie that he couldn't come. By this point I was about sixty, and it would have been silly of me to feel jealous of naked women swimming in the grotto. I couldn't compete with hand-picked twenty-year-olds when I was twenty, so why deny Freddie the pleasure of feeding his fantasies? In the long run, it could only benefit me because I certainly wasn't going to leave him there without my supervision! (Not to mention the supervision of a gay friend, Greg Willenborg, who was there with us.)

Jealousy is a problem in many relationships. One spouse or the other overreacts when their partner shows some interest in someone else of the opposite sex. In fact, many people grow jealous of their partner's fantasy lovers. That's a big mistake. After years of being together, many people need fantasy to become sufficiently aroused for sex . . . with their partner! As long as your partner is having sex only with you, it doesn't matter what is going on in his or her head. Joie de vivre requires you to allow your partner to have as much joy as you do. Maybe you have fantasies or maybe you don't. But trying to control what is going on inside your partner's head is just not a viable strategy. Making them feel guilty about their thoughts won't spread joie de vivre; it will stifle it.

I understand there are some people, mostly women, who have body-image problems. They've put on some weight, maybe after having had a few children, and it lowers their self-esteem. Such a reaction is certainly going to take away from one's joie de vivre. The first key to solving such issues is, as I just said, not to pretend you know what is going on in your partner's mind. Maybe he's fantasizing about the latest rail-thin supermodel, or maybe he's telling the truth when he says he likes your added curves. Keep in mind that larger thighs may be accompanied by larger breasts, which may be more his focus. If you look at old paintings, those curves of yours were once the ideal. They may not be what Madison Avenue chooses to focus on, but that doesn't mean your partner's innate appetites are controlled by what flashes on various screens. He may have a natural inclination to appreciate more in a woman than less.

It's also important for a woman with a body-image problem not to try to keep covered up or have sex only in the dark. Many men need some visual stimulation to become aroused. Take that away from them and you might be creating a self-fulfilling prophesy— that is, a dying sex life—not because of your added weight but your reaction to it.

If you want to feel joie de vivre, it will help for you to live it. So parade your body in front of your partner, show it off, try to feel good about it, and see how he reacts. (And I'd say the same to men who are overweight.) That's not to say that there aren't good reasons to try to reduce your weight. There are health considerations to being overweight that shouldn't be ignored. But while you're working on your weight to become as healthy as possible, don't become obsessed with it.

My marriage to Fred lasted almost thirty-six years and ended only because Fred passed away at far too young an age in 1997. Fred was in good health and an avid skier, but he suffered a stroke and wound up in Columbia Presbyterian Hospital, in Washington Heights. In part because of who his wife was, he was put in the luxury wing and received the best possible care. When I wasn't by his side, I would go to the lounge area, which was beautifully lit by the light pouring in from huge skylights and filled with the music of a professional piano player seated at a grand piano. See what I mean about it being luxurious? But I didn't have too much time to enjoy the surroundings because not only was I worried about Fred, but at the time I was busy reading the galleys of *Sex for Dummies*, which had to be approved under a tight deadline.

Under the wonderful care of Dr. Stephan Mayer, Fred recovered from that stroke and eventually even went back to work, which was very important to him, as it made him both happy and proud to be able to continue to lead a useful and productive life. Then he had another stroke. I'd been out at an Oscar party. I called him to say I was on my way home and he said he was fine. When I arrived, I found him sitting up in bed. He said to me, "Ruth, help me. Another stroke. I have a bad headache."

I called 9-1-1, and he was taken back to Columbia. Dr. Mayer rushed to the hospital, as I had called him too, but this time there was no recovery. Fred never uttered another word. Ten days later, he passed away. And I graduated from being an orphan to being a widow—a much tougher role. A child is resilient, while an older adult is less so. A child is supposed to break away from her parents at some point, and even at the age of ten, some of the seeds of independence are already sown. Unlike a child halfway out the door, in a good marriage, with every passing day you're in more deeply.

"Go out and be active," is what I would tell anyone in the situation I found myself in, but I know how hard that can be. Luckily I was already a celebrity, so I was able to engage in all the distractions I needed rather than just mope around in an empty apartment.

When each day's mail brings more invitations to events than you can possibly attend, it's much easier to just dive into that river of social activity and let it float you away from your misery.

There are so many kinds of tears, and you can cry many of them all at the same time. When I was on that train all those years ago, having no idea what the future held for the German Jews left behind, I was crying partially out of frustration. I hadn't wanted to go to Heiden; I'd wanted to stay with my parents and grandmother, so I felt that I'd been treated unfairly. I was lonely, so that brought on tears too. I was afraid of what this school I was going to would be like. I'd given away the one doll I'd brought, and now I missed it and all my other toys. And I missed each of my family members in a different way, so remembering my grandmother's hugs brought on a different set of emotions than remembering walking to synagogue with my father. And while I was only ten, I'd witnessed the wrath of the Nazis against the Jews. I'd seen the burned-out hulk of our synagogue. I'd seen all the shop windows shattered. And I'd seen my father taken away by black-booted soldiers. I was afraid for my family more so than I was afraid for myself, but I also felt guilty that I had left them behind to face the Nazis without me. So I had more than my share of reasons to cry.

Have you ever been faced with a sad situation and tried to hold back your tears? Because there are so many sources for each tear, it's hard. You force back one emotion only to get hit by another. So you stuff them into some interior closet—but then when you need your emotions, you discover they're locked up, out of your reach. When you want to love someone, you can't, because not only is the sadness hidden away, but so is every other emotion along with it. And the longer this goes on, the more terrified you become of the flood of emotions that might erupt were you to unlock that door. So crying and letting the emotions out is a good thing and actively promotes joie de vivre. That I was only ten and without the resources to keep those tears at bay ended up helping me to cope. Because over time, rather than try to lock up all my emotions, I learned to keep some under wraps while releasing others, which allowed me to be able to love, laugh, and cry as I continued on through my life.

CHAPTER VI

Enjoy the Crazy Turns Life Takes

What started me on the path to stardom was losing my job. The School of Hard Knocks has a lot to offer in terms of upward mobility, though during class you're probably going to feel more like a failure than a rising star. And very often, you're at the top of your game when failure happens, which makes the fall that much worse. For example, one time when this happened to me, I was one of the most popular professors and my classes were full to the brim. The head of the department was having problems getting enough students to sign up for her class, which should have made me watch my back; but as often happens, I never saw that blow coming. Yet as miserable as I felt staring at that pink slip, it gave me the freedom a bit later on to accept the offer that led to that pink cover of *People!* So you never know.

Talking about Sex Isn't So Crazy

In 1967 the money ran out for the public health project I was working on, and that left me out of a job. I began asking around for leads and was told that Planned Parenthood was looking for a research associate. I applied and not only did I get the job, but a week later the man who was running the project quit and I got his job! My bad luck had turned to good luck.

My role was to train and supervise two dozen women as paraprofessionals who were to be sent out to collect the contraception and abortion histories of about two thousand women in Harlem.

At the end of my first day, I came home and said to my husband, Fred: "These people are crazy! All they talk about all day long is sex!" About a week later, though, I decided that they weren't so crazy and sex was a topic with which I wanted a closer relationship. Like most people, I considered sex to be a private matter—and I still do—but it also became obvious that people needed help with their sex lives, and providing that help was a true calling.

Today, because I now talk about sex all day long myself, many people assume that my views on the subject have undergone a radical transformation, that I've become some sort of libertine who thinks that any type of sex done any which way with anybody is perfectly fine. While it's true I know a lot more about what goes on in people's bedrooms than I did back then, my overall perspective isn't much different. As I say over and over again, I am old-fashioned and a square. I want people *in a relationship* to have the best sex possible, but I'm not in favor of some of these modern sexual practices such as "friends with benefits." I bring this up because if you thought making this decision to go into the field of sex came easily to me, you'd be wrong. My background as an Orthodox Jew raised in Germany was a very conservative one. That marriage manual was in a locked cabinet, remember? Sex was not a subject that was bandied about in the home where I grew up. And one reason for that was the manner in which I came into the world.

My paternal grandmother had engaged my mother to be a housekeeper. Nowhere in the job description had there been any mention of having sex with her son, but that's what happened. And since they didn't use contraceptives, one of those unintended pregnancies that I preach against morning, noon, and night took place, and I was the result. It's an ironic twist, but it doesn't change my opinion that contraceptive use is important. Maybe that attitude was instilled in me by my grandmother because she was somewhat cold toward my mother, and the reason was clearly based on the manner in which I was conceived. So given my upbringing, though I've been a sex therapist for many years now, I still sometimes blush when talking about sex in public.

People who are sexually frustrated will find it harder to find joie de vivre in their lives, but there is a difference between understanding how to achieve sexual satisfaction and being completely open about sex. How you were raised does affect your attitude toward sex. Some people can come from a home where sex was a topic that was never discussed and learn to be more open-minded, while others from such a background always have difficulty with the subject. But you can be a very private person and still have orgasms. Your life doesn't have to be an open book in order to find sexual satisfaction. It's true that as part of a couple, the more openly you can discuss your sex life with your partner, the better the communication, the better your sex life is likely to be. But there are many couples that don't talk about sex, and yet both halves of the couple find satisfaction in their sex lives.

To enjoy joie de vivre, you have to be comfortable in your own skin. You can't allow your limitations to strangle you. Again, if your background was so prudish that it prevents you from experiencing sexual satisfaction, I would strongly urge you to go for professional help. But if you're very conservative when it comes to sex but do have orgasms regularly, then don't worry about it. You can expand your horizons in other ways, intellectually and physically.

At Planned Parenthood, I was only supposed to train the women going out into the field, but I wanted to see how my training was being used. So sometimes I'd accompany them when they went out to take surveys. The streets of East Harlem weren't the safest place back in those days, and the insides of some buildings were in worse condition than the streets. Climbing all those stairs—remember, stairs are more of an obstacle for me than for most people—smelling the urine, and stepping around the garbage sometimes made me wonder if I had made the right decision not to stay back in the office. However, listening to these young women tell their tales opened my eyes. I'd known poverty, but because I had ten good years with my family, my foundation was solid. Most of the young women we interviewed were facing the world completely on their own. Even though they were sexually active, many didn't have the slightest idea of the connection between what they were doing and the potential consequences.

The women I sent out were only supposed to ask questions, but often I couldn't stop myself from adding some advice. I remember sitting in the living room of one young mother of three. The plaster at the corner of the ceiling was coming down in chunks, the table had to lean against the wall because it had only three legs, and the green couch we were sitting on was terribly stained. I asked her about the father of her children, and while she knew who two were, she wasn't so sure about the third. And, of course, none of them were helping her in any way.

"Do you have a partner now?" I asked.

"Yes," she replied.

"Do you use contraceptives?"

"No."

"Why not?"

"He says he doesn't like condoms."

"Do you want another child?" I asked her, looking into her eyes. Her only response was to look down at the floor.

I explained the options to her, though I could tell that having that fourth baby was probably inevitable without some intervention. It made me sad, but at least the program I was working on might help bring women like her some assistance.

My next job was as a professor at Lehman College in the Bronx. There my specialty became instructing teachers and prospective teachers how to conduct classes on sex education. Because of my "expertise," I was suddenly being asked very specific questions about sex by both students and fellow faculty members. Students would take a long time packing up their books so they'd be the last one to leave the classroom, and they'd come up to me and ask questions such as, "Professor, does the pull-out method really work?" or, "My boyfriend and I have sex, but I've never had an orgasm." I usually gave them an answer of sorts, but often it was based on common sense, not hard facts. I wanted to be able to help them more knowledgably, which led me to decide to become better educated.

When I first came to the States and needed to learn English quickly, I turned to reading the *True Confessions*-type of magazines. The language was simple enough for me to grasp and the stories entertaining enough to hold my attention. But while these magazines certainly covered sex—adventurous sex at that—now I needed something with more depth. My first foray into getting an academic background was a week's worth of seminars given by Long Island Jewish Hospital. I learned a lot, but this wasn't a long-term solution. I then read on a bulletin board that the famed sex therapist Dr. Helen Singer Kaplan was giving a lecture at the Ford Foundation. I bought a ticket and off I went.

The auditorium was packed, but I had arrived early because I knew that if I didn't get a seat down toward the front, I wouldn't be able to see a thing. After Dr. Kaplan spoke, she showed a couple of short films. Then there was a question-and-answer session. I was determined to ask a question, but the audience was composed mostly of other experts. My heart was racing as I tried to think of a question that wouldn't make it obvious how little I knew but would still be interesting.

"Dr. Kaplan, do you believe that premature ejaculation is more readily treatable if the man has a partner?" That set off a discussion among the audience. After the lecture, I approached Dr. Kaplan while she was still at the podium. Dr. Kaplan complimented me on my question, which gave me the courage to ask her if I could visit her training program for sex therapists at Cornell Medical School. She gave me a smile and said, "Of course." That was a Thursday, and on the next Tuesday I showed up. As you may have discovered, I'm a very impatient person!

Impatience may not be a virtue, but if you constantly procrastinate, that's going to limit the amount of joie de vivre you experience. Each of us is given only a limited amount of time on this earth, and we don't know when the ticker inside of us is going to stop, so wasting time is a big mistake. I understand that if you're supposed to do something unpleasant, you might put if off—but you know what? Those types of chores somehow always manage to get done because there's a need. But you don't have to see the latest movie or feel the sun on your face that first warm spring day, so it's all too easy to just sigh and miss out on these pleasures. But if you keep putting off everything that can bring pleasure, then your life becomes dull. So when it comes to joie de vivre, stop procrastinating and instead make enjoying life to the fullest a priority.

For the next three months, I was a regular visitor at Dr. Kaplan's program. The more I learned auditing those classes, the more I realized that being a sex therapist was the right career choice for me. Sex therapy appealed to me because of my impatient nature. It's a form of behavioral therapy in which the patient doesn't have to spend a long time looking for the root cause of their problem but instead gets instruction on what to do right away to improve their situation.

Let me give you an example. Many men complain of not being able to last long enough during intercourse. The condition is called premature ejaculation, or PE. (You may remember it was the subject of the question I asked Dr. Kaplan during her lecture.) It's not a physical ailment; it's more of a learning disability. One theory behind the condition is that young men masturbating behind a locked bathroom or bedroom door train themselves to reach orgasm quickly, in the event that a family member comes a-knocking. As a result, they are then stuck in an instant-gratification mode, which is not so desirable when they begin to have sex with a partner. But as a sex therapist, you don't care why your client has PE. You don't undertake a psychological dig to find out when and how a client masturbated or whether or not he was attracted to his fourth-grade teacher. Your job as a sex therapist is to teach him how to gain the control he is seeking. And that can be done in a rather short time. You assign your client homework—and if he does it properly (even better is if he has a partner willing to work with him), he can gain control over his ejaculations in a few weeks' time. Much of a sex therapist's advice is of a similar nature. It's short, moves quickly, and gets results. Just like me!

I made up my mind and enrolled in Dr. Kaplan's program as a student. Remember I said I was old-fashioned and a square? Well, for me to conduct sexual-status examinations of those who came to the clinic, asking them every last detail about their sex lives, was not easy. With some clients (since we're not medical doctors, we call them clients, not patients), all the details would spill out without much prompting, but others needed coaxing.

"So, you gave your husband oral sex last night. Did he ejaculate in your mouth?"

Just because you use a medical term like "ejaculate" rather than "come," or as young people these days spell it, "cum," doesn't make it any easier. Especially as a good sex therapist has to picture in her mind exactly what a client is doing when having sex. (And that's the reason that I don't treat people who are into bestiality or S&M.) But in time I learned to overcome my natural reticence to pry into people's sex lives and could even smile when I thought of the "homework" my patients were doing in their bedrooms. After two years of training, I got a certificate from Cornell as a psychosexual therapist. That one went right up on my wall. And I quickly started to develop a private practice.

As a leading figure in the field of sex therapy, Dr. Kaplan was bombarded with speaking requests. Since she couldn't accept most of them, other members of the faculty sometimes took her place. One day Dr. Kaplan received a letter saying that the managers of the community affairs departments of the New York radio stations were looking for someone to address them, and I volunteered. I often did, as I believed not only in the importance of what we sex therapists were doing, but also that by meeting lots of new people, other doors might open up for me.

I was more nervous than usual during the elevator ride up to the ballroom at the St. Moritz Hotel, but I can't say that I had any premonition of where this fifteen-minute talk was going to lead.

While I had this group of radio station executives in my hot little hands, I decided to float a trial balloon, never actually imagining that it would soar to the heights it did. I told them that we need more sex education in this country and that radio stations, as significant others, had a duty to help spread correct sexual information to their listeners. One of the managers attending, Betty Elam of WYNY-FM, asked for my card, and a few days later called me with an offer to appear on one of her station's community affairs programs. And so I was interviewed by Mitch Lebe. Poor Mitch, a longtime reporter on the New York airwaves, had to be forced by Betty to take on this assignment. His show was on at ten o'clock on Sunday morning, and the last topic he wanted to cover was sex. But somehow he managed to get through it, and as a result of that interview, on May 5, 1980, Betty offered me a fifteen-minute slot on Sunday nights at twelve fifteen a.m.

For my first show, which was taped on a Tuesday afternoon, I just spoke about my philosophy, but I asked listeners to write in their questions and they soon came pouring in. After that I would read the letters over the air and then answer the questions. When the station's program director, Maurice Tunick, said to me, "You're going to be the talk of the town," not only did I not understand the reference to the *New Yorker* column, but I didn't believe him. After all, my little show was airing at such a late hour on a Sunday night that I found it hard to believe many people were actually listening. One early indicator of how my show was catching on was from people who recognized my voice. The first time it happened was when I gave a coin to a blind man begging on the street while adding some comment, and he said, "Thank you, Dr. Ruth." Then taxi drivers started to recognize me once I spoke up. Since I was on radio, nobody knew what I looked like, but my unique accent seemed easy to pick up.

(At this point, I have to jump ahead to tell you a story. When I first came to this country it was suggested that I get a voice coach to lose—or at least reduce—my accent, which is a rather unique mixture of the accents from places I've lived, including Germany, Israel, and France. While I didn't think it was a bad idea, I couldn't afford it, so it was out of the question. When Debra Jo Rupp, who starred as the mom in *That '70 s Show*, was engaged to play me in the theater production *Becoming Dr. Ruth*, the first thing she did was hire a coach to teach her my accent! I get such a kick out of that.)

Most of WYNY's programming wasn't talk, but music, and the "stars" of the station were the DJs. The station had engaged an outside

PR firm to make it better known, and the young man who was handling the account was looking for angles to generate stories in the press. When he was told there was a sex therapist hosting a show, he asked to see me.

That PR person was Pierre Lehu, whose name you can see on the front cover of this book. I later started to call him my minister of communications. In addition to handling my public relations, he also became my coauthor on many books, and he helps me keep my life together. When my children want to know where I am, they know the best way to find out is to call Pierre.

The firm he worked for was based in a converted apartment, and his office was what had once been the kitchen, so its walls were filled with shelves and cabinets.

"Dr. Westheimer, to generate press interest I need an angle, a hook. Is there anything you've done lately that's a bit different than other sex therapists?"

I have to admit I was a bit surprised by his question. I told him about the class for disabled students that I had conducted at Brooklyn College.

"This class was so inspirational, and I learned as much from my students as they learned from me. It was so fabulous that I will never do it again."

"Why not?" asked Pierre with a confused look on his face. (I have an obligation to Pierre, a promise I made to him, to make him laugh once a day, but over the years I've also often left him wondering what hit him!)

"Because by mixing the two groups, the able and the disabled, they both learn valuable lessons from one another. I don't know that we could replicate the magic of that class again."

He liked that angle, but my initial reaction to the result wasn't so positive. When he called to say that a reporter from the *New York*

Daily News wanted to interview me, I was horrified. I was a college professor, and the *New York Times* was my bible. How could I appear in a tabloid like the *Daily News*? It would ruin my reputation. As it turned out, the reporter was a Harvard graduate, which impressed me, and the article was just perfect.

Pierre got me some other local media, and my growing notoriety gave me the courage to ask Betty for more airtime with live call-ins. I made an appointment to meet with her after one of my Tuesday taping sessions at Rockefeller Center. We met in her office (which was on the small side, as community-affairs programming wasn't much of a revenue producer).

"Betty, the letters are just pouring in, and you've seen all the press I've been getting."

In her soft-spoken way, she replied, "Of course, Ruth, who hasn't? I think the DJs are getting jealous."

"I'd like to make them even more jealous. I'd like to have a longer show with live call-ins."

Betty thought about that for a minute. It was one thing to have a sex therapist talking about sex late at night; at an earlier hour, younger people might be listening. And with live call-ins, now the public would be on the air, and they might say things that were inappropriate.

"I'll have to ask Frank," she finally replied, passing the buck to Frank Osborn, the station manager. And I later found out he had to go up the chain of command to various executives at NBC to clear the idea. But as I said, it was hard getting commercials for community-affairs shows, and if my show became popular, then the ad dollars would flow in—and so the powers that be gave their OK. Only now it was *my* turn to throw a monkey wrench into the negotiations. I asked for a meeting to speak with Frank in his big corner office. He asked me to sit down, but at my height, I prefer to stand. In fact, I circled around to his side of the desk where he was sitting and stood next to him, so that I was the one with the height advantage, though only barely—Frank is a tall guy.

"Frank," I said, putting my hand on his shoulder, "I know that my new show will have commercials. That's great but I can't have any abortion clinics taking ads."

I believe that abortion must remain legal, but I understood that there would be those who would be upset about this little German professor talking openly about sex on radio, and I knew that if there were also ads for abortion clinics during my hour, the opposition might come down so hard that the show would soon be off the air.

"Ruth, I think you're right about that. I'll tell the sales department that they have to clear all ads through me, and if anything that I think you might not approve crosses my desk, I'll check with you."

And so in September 1981, *Sexually Speaking* started broadcasting live at ten p.m. on Sunday nights. I was given a producer to screen the calls, Susan Brown, who was just perfect. She was a young Catholic who blushed very easily, exactly the type of person needed to run interference. I was going to be using very frank language that no one else on radio was using—words like *penis, vagina, orgasm,* and *masturbation.* Clearly that would give some people the wrong idea, and it would be up to Susan to spot callers who wanted to push the envelope too far. If someone used a banned four-letter word, my program was on a seven-second delay, and I had a big yellow kill button in front of me so that I could cut off anything inappropriate before it went out over the airwaves. Actually I almost never had to use it—which is a good thing, because I don't have the fastest reflexes!

That I was able to break this new ground was the result of a combination of factors. First, there was my training. I wasn't trying to shock but rather educate. Then, because of my conservative background, I was careful not to titillate. That I was an older woman also helped people accept this talk from me. I think too that my accent gave me a certain authority I might not have had otherwise. In part because of my accent, the *New York Times* dubbed me Grandma Freud. I wasn't yet a grandma, nor ever a psychiatrist, but to some degree that description sums up well why my talking about sex on radio was acceptable.

Speaking of names, it seems that listeners couldn't pronounce or remember Westheimer, so when they called in they started calling me simply Dr. Ruth. The media picked it up, and I lost the use of my last name.

With the live radio show, media coverage exploded. I graduated from print coverage to TV, first with appearances on local New York stations and then on national shows like *The Late Show with David Letterman* and *The Tonight Show Starring Johnny Carson*. Johnny even had a special chair built for me so that when I sat down, a footrest slid out for my feet. (Later he started a comedy bit where he pretended to be me and I was never on the show with him again, though I was when Joan Rivers hosted.) And then, as mentioned, I was on the cover of *People* magazine and I became, literally, a household name.

Of all the talk-show appearances I've made over the years, the one that undoubtedly got the biggest laugh occurred on *David Letterman*. Dave asked me if I'd received any interesting questions lately. I said a young man had called in not with a question but a comment. He said that his girlfriend liked to toss onion rings over his erect penis. The audience immediately began to howl, and Dave pretended to be outraged, stood up, and walked offstage. The guest after me was the baseball pitcher Tug McGraw, who kept mentioning onion rings in his end of the conversation, eliciting more laughter. And the audience at home got to play along as the producers quickly put together a picture of a plate of onion rings that they flashed at each station break. They continued to use that image each time I was on *Letterman*, and people still bring up that show to me all the time.

I recognize that with such a story, I was pushing my own boundary lines, being more of a comedienne than a sex therapist. But first of all, this was a real story, not a joke that I made up. And the truth is, the more entertaining I was, the more I was asked back—and the better I could push the important messages I had to give. I'm old-fashioned and a square, but I'm not dumb!

In fact, I'm not good at telling actual jokes. And yet I can make people laugh, whether in large groups or one-on-one. Much of that ability comes from my spirit. I don't go around with a long face; usually I'm smiling. At what? I actually look for things to smile about. If I'm going to a concert later that night and I start to feel in a bad mood, I think about the wonderful melodies I'll be hearing later. I make a conscious effort to be positive. And if you want the most joie de vivre in your life, that's what you must do as well. Negative thoughts will pop into your head, as they do to me and everybody. But why give in to those thoughts and allow your mood to be dragged downward? My suggestion is to fight off the temptation to go negative and work at being positive. Try it out and see what happens. I'm willing to bet you find the experience worth repeating again and again.

While I enjoyed being recognized by people as I walked down the street, or having the men on fire and garbage trucks honk and wave as they drove by, the reason I appreciated being a celebrity was that it allowed me to communicate my messages about safer sex to a much wider audience. As proud as I am of what I've done, more importantly I helped open the door for the spread of reliable information about sex across every possible avenue. Today you'll hear and see discussions about every sexual topic in every medium. Of course, some of this information is erroneous, and that's the downside of popularizing the topic of sex. But some of the basic messages—such as using condoms to protect yourself against the spread of disease—have gone viral, and that's a good thing. Teenage pregnancy rates are down, and that's in part because so many more teens got the message about the importance of condom use.

While I ask the most personal questions of people who come to my office with a sex problem, I never ask a personal question in public. That's not to say that people don't ask *me* personal questions in public. I especially have a hard time going to the ladies' room in restaurants and theaters because I'm often cornered by some woman who desperately needs my advice. Sometimes I give them a quick answer. Other times, I smile sweetly and say, "Sorry, but I can't help you." If I'm out with another woman, very often I ask her to accompany me to the ladies' room just to protect me!

Vera Wang

The following story emphasizes how I operate. Pierre was going to a party to celebrate his fortieth high school reunion; since he knew I wasn't busy that night, he asked me if I wanted to go. Under normal circumstances, I wouldn't go to a private affair like this, but it turns out that Vera Wang had been a member of his class, and the party was to be held at her fabulous Park Avenue apartment. I love my apartment in Washington Heights for its great views of the Hudson River, but it's not quite up to the type of place I imagined Vera to have. Plus it would give me the chance to meet some of Pierre's friends and learn more about him. And so I accepted.

The apartment was well worth the visit—vast rooms filled with exquisite furniture, all very tastefully done, which you'd expect from a fashion icon. I'd met Vera several times at functions where the famous gather, but our relationship was of the air-kiss variety. Seeing her in this environment, interacting with her old friends, allowed me to see a side of this famous fashion designer that I otherwise would not have been privy to.

It was late spring of 2007, a time when my life was in flux. I'd had an office in a building on 73rd Street and Lexington Avenue devoted to the medical profession for twenty-some odd years, but the owners decided they wanted to turn it into co-ops, and so they gave us all the boot—with only thirty days' notice. That was ridiculous on so many counts, especially since it took them years to get the work started, and so they lost out on all that rent. But while some in the building wanted to hire a lawyer to fight the evictions in court, that's not my style. If they didn't want me, I didn't want to be there. Thus I spread the word that Dr. Ruth was about to be homeless—or at least that's how I put it.

One woman who was attending the party, Leslie Rahl, had remained loyal to the island of Manhattan. When she heard my tale of woe—and believe me, I was telling everyone, because you never know—she said: "Dr. Ruth, I can't have you homeless. I have extra space in my office, so I want you to move in with me."

You know how some people say they jump up and down for joy but they never really move a muscle? I actually jumped up and down. It's not that I couldn't have found space, but the whole process of looking was one I didn't have time for. And when I went to see Leslie's offices, they were fabulous—high up, with great views of the Chrysler Building. I've been with Leslie ever since, and when she moved, she took me with her, even putting my name on the lease, though she doesn't charge me. All she wants is that I bring with me my joie de vivre. She says my energy and good spirits are worth more than any money I could pay her, and who am I to disagree? I make sure to take her out to lunch regularly, and if she asks me to go to a charity fund-raiser, I'm there. But when I say it's good to be Dr. Ruth, in this instance no one would disagree.

And that leads me to one last story for this chapter. I was in the Sea Grill, a restaurant where I often go, and one of the waiters took me aside to tell me that he'd heard me talk about testicular cancer and the importance of self-examination. He'd examined himself, found a lump, and went to see a doctor, and it turned out that it had been cancer. He credited me for saving his life. Helping people in this way was exactly the reason I'd wanted to become a doctor as a young woman. It doesn't happen to me every day, but I know that I've saved some people's lives and helped a lot more in other ways by preventing them from getting a disease or having an unintended pregnancy. And to me, that's what is really important about being Dr. Ruth. Fame came to me late enough in life that if I'd never ridden in a limousine or attended a premier or had any of the other perks that come with celebrity, I would have been fine. It's fun, but I never let it go to my head. But what does give me immense satisfaction is that I've been able to help so many people in important ways. Not the least of which is by teaching them to have *terrrrific* sex!

When I was ten, I'd wanted to be a doctor. Maybe at that age I didn't know exactly what that meant, but I knew I wanted to help people. The joy that one can find in giving—be it money or assistance or maybe even just your ear to someone in need of one—cannot be matched by any other means. There's the joy of sex, the joy of success, the joy of acquiring an object you desire—but the satisfaction that comes with giving is a very powerful emotion that you can't get any other way. So if you want to experience joie de vivre in all its forms, you have to be open to giving of yourself. You don't have to be a saint and give every second of every day, but you also shouldn't be a miser, because the person you'll be cheating the most is yourself.

CHAPTER VII

How Celebrity Influenced My Life—and Could Influence Yours

I began my journey to earning the title of Dr. Ruth on radio, but it was television that really made me a household name, first with guest appearances on such national shows as *The Tonight Show, David Letterman,* and *Today,* and then on my own shows. When I was merely a guest with a segment that was no more than five minutes on the subject of sex, the time flew by; these shows were easy to do. But when I had my own show, transforming myself from interviewee to interviewer and having to fill thirty or sixty minutes with entertaining television . . . that was more of a challenge. And one reason was how little I knew of American pop culture.

Having grown up in four different countries before finally settling in the States—and not being one to watch much TV when I did move here—if I had to take a test in American popular culture, I'd be the first one to admit that I'd fail, which is a bit ironic when you think that I've actually had a small part to play in American pop culture. In any case, my lack of knowledge did cause some problems for the producers of my own TV shows, as they had to fully brief me to make sure that I didn't come off sounding like a stranger in my own country.

Let me give you one example. I was having my hair and makeup done before taping one of my shows, and Marsha Lebby, one of the show's producers, was talking to me about one of the guests we were having on the next segment.

"Today's guest is Bianca Jagger."

"Am I supposed to know who that is?" I asked over the sound of the hair dryer.

"She's the ex-wife of Mick Jagger," the producer said, figuring that would tell me all I needed to know.

However, my next question was: "And who is this Mick Jagger?"

See what I mean? What I know about rock music could fill a thimble. And yet I also know some rock stars. U2 thanked me when they received a Grammy one year, used me to do an ad for one of their albums (*Zooropa*), and then invited me to a concert. I went backstage afterward and talked with Bono and the other band members, and Bono gave me a quote for my book *Musically Speaking*. Elton John is a fan of mine. And in the next chapter I'll tell you my Paul McCartney story. So while there are plenty of older people who aren't up on the latest musical trends, few of them actually can say they've met a pop star. But I don't let this dichotomy bother me in the least. I'm sorry I didn't get the chance to meet my music idols, men like Beethoven and Bach, but I am friends with some of the top classical conductors, such as Zubin Mehta, so it's not that I'm culturally illiterate at all. It's just that those I admire are a little long in the tooth, or maybe even not around anymore.

I don't want to leave you with the impression that I can't be starstruck. Before I was very well-known, I dragged Fred to see a Broadway show, *Private Lives*, starring Richard Burton and Elizabeth Taylor. I was such a big fan of Elizabeth Taylor that even though it was raining, I insisted that we wait outside the stage door afterward to get a glimpse of her as she left.

"Ruthie, it's raining, there are all these people out here, so you can't even get close. So why do we have to hang around and get soaking wet?"

"Fred, how many times are you going to see Elizabeth Taylor in person?"

"But I just saw her in person on the stage!"

"Fred, you don't understand."

Maybe if it had been one of Fred's idols, like Tony Randall, he would have been the one dragging me out into a rainy night. In any case, I do think it's special to see celebrities; it's just that who I consider a celebrity doesn't exactly match the opinion of the average American, especially younger ones. And speaking of Ms. Taylor, I did finally get to meet her. There was a big AIDS fund-raiser at the Jacob Javits Center, and I was invited onstage with her for some press pictures before the event began. And she knew who I was! That totally amazed me—again, I knew her from seeing her movies when I was much younger and still a complete nobody. To have Elizabeth Taylor look at me with those violet eyes, smile, and say, "Hi, Dr. Ruth," was just thrilling.

And I haven't lost my admiration for Burton and Taylor. During a recent visit to South Africa, I made sure to visit the church where they got married. So you see, I can be as starstruck as anyone else. Just not about Mick Jagger!

Fantasy

Many people fantasize about famous people. And when I talk fantasy, I mean that in their heads they have sex with their idols. In my opinion, that's fine, at least to a point. (More on that in a minute.) If you've been with the same person for a long time, sometimes your libido needs a little boost, and using fantasy is one way to achieve that. Also, if your head is filled with negative thoughts that impede your ability to become sexually aroused—say you have a boss that's always making nasty comments that you play over and over in your head, including when you're in bed with your partner—substituting a fantasy about your favorite celebrity can help you to push those nasty thoughts aside so that you can have sex with your partner. So using fantasy appropriately is one way to enjoy life a little more.

On the other hand, fantasizing about your next-door neighbor can be problematic. The reason is that when you fantasize about a celebrity, the odds of that fantasy ever coming true are almost zero, so those fantasies don't pose any danger to your actual relationship. But if you're fantasizing about the guy or gal next door, well, the possibility of acting out on that fantasy can drive an imaginary or actual wedge between you and your partner. Better to fantasize about famous unobtainable people rather than someone who might take you up on turning your fantasy into a reality!

The problem with giving advice is that there's often an exception that proves your advice wrong, at least if pushed to its limits. I knew a young woman who asked me to introduce her to Jerry Seinfeld. She had a serious crush on him and wanted to turn her fantasies into reality. Now, I'd had Jerry as a guest on my TV show a couple of times, but it's not as if we were friends. But more important, this young women wasn't his type, and he didn't need any help from me in finding dates. Her problem was that she *did* need such help. By entering so deeply into her fantasy world that she lost track of reality, she was making that process of finding a partner even more difficult. So while fantasy can help with joie de vivre, if pushed to the extreme as with this young woman's case, it can also be damaging. With everything in life, moderation more often than not is the key to actually getting the most out of life.

∼

Because of my specialty, when I use the term "faking it," most people jump to the conclusion that I'm talking about faking it in bed. And of course in that sense, I do talk about it quite often. When it comes to sex, I tell women not to fake orgasms—or at least, not regularly. Once in a while if they're tired, then it's OK. But if they never reveal to their partner that they're not getting sexual satisfaction but instead always fake having orgasms, that's a big problem. It can lead to a severe problem when it comes to fulfilling your requirements for joie de vivre, as sexual satisfaction is an important component of that. But here I'd like to cover the topic of faking it in other contexts, because I say that when you're not in the bedroom but out in society, it's all right to fake it when needed. And since I'm often being introduced to people I don't know (even if I should), I've become quite good at it.

Since the point of faking is not to let the other person know that you have no idea of who they are, it's an art that you have to practice to get good at. And I get a lot of practice because I meet so many people that it's impossible for me to remember them all. When someone comes up to me and starts talking to me as if they're my oldest friend, I just go with the flow of conversation and hope for the best. If they say something that triggers a memory and I realize who they are, then I keep talking. On the other hand, if after a minute or so I realize that even if I shook their hand ten years ago at a party, the connection is no deeper than that, I smile, say, "Excuse me," and walk away.

Of course, sometimes I'm in the shoes of the person I just mentioned. Someone comes up to me and I can tell that they're famous, but I have no idea who they are. But they know me—if not because we've met before, at least they know I'm Dr. Ruth. At a movie opening, for example, I know the room is full of celebrities, but I don't know most of them. So what do I do? Smile a lot, pose for pictures with them, and then, when they walk away . . . ask someone else who they were. Fortunately, at most of these events, the conversations never get very deep; the risk of saying the wrong thing is minor. And if it's a party after a movie opening, then at least I know who the stars of the movie are!

But when I was taping my TV shows, I wasn't supposed to fake it. On camera I had to appear at least as knowledgeable as my audience. However, when you've done 495 shows and you're "celebrity handicapped," that can be difficult. Luckily for me, in a TV studio there were always "faking aids" for the host, cards held up next to the camera or a teleprompter giving me the questions I needed to ask (though despite having these, sometimes my producer, John Lollos, was left scrambling, shouting last-minute instructions into the earpiece of the stage manager, Dean Gordon, to make sure I asked the right follow-up question!).

Most of my shows aired on Lifetime Television, though they seemed to change titles regularly. *The Dr. Ruth Show* was first. Then I jumped to a syndicated show that also aired in some other countries, including England and Hong Kong. It was called *Ask Dr. Ruth*. Then I went back to Lifetime for *The All New Dr. Ruth Show*, which was followed by *What's Up, Dr. Ruth?* The purpose of that show, aimed at teens, was to broaden Lifetime's appeal to the younger set. Then they changed the format again, and it was called *You're on the Air with Dr. Ruth*. In the fall of 1992, I moved to Nostalgia Television with a show called *Never Too Late*.

We had some really interesting and funny guests over the years, including Burt Reynolds, George Burns, Milton Berle, Jerry Lewis, Jerry Seinfeld, Howie Mandel, Cyndi Lauper, Bill Cosby, Isaac Asimov, Regis Philbin, Mayor Ed Koch, Gloria Steinem, Helen Gurley Brown,

Martin Scorsese, Joan Rivers, and many, many more. You can see parts of some of these interviews on my YouTube channel.

When Roseanne Barr came on my show, she wasn't a big star with her own show yet. She was a stand-up comedienne and she was funny, but when she sat down next to me, I could see she was chewing gum. Under some circumstances I could have faked it and pretended that I hadn't seen what she was doing, but this was my TV set—and I had no intention of letting her off the hook.

"Roseanne, I'm a teacher and I look at this set as if it was my classroom, and one rule I've always had in my classroom is no chewing gum."

Roseanne is rarely at a loss for words, but she looked at me and was speechless. I offered her a tissue; she took it and spat out her gum, and we had a wonderful interview after that. And after all these years, I know she remembers that episode. When I was having difficulty getting my Twitter account verified, someone told me that Roseanne had had the same difficulties, so I contacted her via Twitter. She answered me and mentioned the gum incident. She wasn't able to help me, but it made me smile to think of Roseanne remembering me telling her she couldn't chew gum on my set. (Eventually someone else put me in touch with someone at Twitter, and I was awarded my blue star.) So you see, standing up for your principles is one way of making your life more enjoyable—and memorable.

I'd also like to suggest that you absorb the fact that in your life, you're the central character, the celebrity. When approaching a major birthday, many people will say, "Oh, I don't want anyone to make a fuss. I don't need a party." But imagine how miserable you'd feel if this birthday slipped by and nobody noticed! So if you do need to have this birthday marked, you might as well give yourself permission to enjoy it like the celebrity you are for the day.

Why do some people not get even a fraction of the joie de vivre that others do? Because they feel they don't deserve it. They put themselves down, say that they're not important. But nobody is more important in your life than you! And rather than push joy away, you have to reach out your two hands and grab it whenever possible. When a celebrity walks down the red carpet, she expects to be photographed. Think of your life like a red carpet, put a smile on your face and accept whatever attention you can get and enjoy it. Sure, if you keep your head down and let your hair cover your face, you won't get the notice you deserve and all that inattention will make you miserable. In life there are no half measures. You can't expect to be given a pat on the back if you run away from every outstretched hand. So think of yourself as the celebrity you are and accept whatever glory comes your way.

If you look at the list of famous guests on my shows, you'll note that many were comedians. That wasn't an accident, because comedians are consistently entertaining—their quick wits give them the ability to find a joke no matter what the subject, and with sex, it's even easier. Now, I didn't book the show; that was up to John and his associates. But while comedians might make fun of the advice I gave, I also kept in mind what the Talmud says, that a lesson learned with humor is one retained. So if together these comedians and I could make the audience laugh while also providing some useful information about sex, then I was quite satisfied.

I hope you realize that when you are watching an interview, there's a lot of faking going on. It may appear as if the conversation is spontaneous, but in fact both the host and the guest are well prepared so that there is no "dead air"—no awkward moments of silence—and also so that the conversation is always entertaining. And to some extent, my advice is to prepare for any conversation you might have the same way. If you're meeting a friend for lunch, read the morning papers so that you're up on the latest news. If you're up watching late night TV the night before and hear a funny joke, write it down so that you're prepared to repeat it at lunch.

Mining the joie de vivre that life has to offer requires that you put some effort into what you do. It's all right to have some "dead air" during a lunch, but you don't want there to be too much of it, and you want the overall atmosphere to be one where you both come away feeling good about having gotten together. If you provide entertaining conversation, then people will want to get together with you. But if you're boring, then you'll find yourself alone more and more, and that's not going to provide you with a very rich life.

Of course, even comedians have their softer side. I remember George Burns telling me how, after Gracie died, he continued to sleep on the same side of the bed. He got sort of misty-eyed, and you could see how much he'd loved her. It was moments like these that proved why having someone who was a therapist in the host's chair was so valuable. Guests would sometimes forget that they were on television and open up to me in ways they never would if the host were another comedian. When you're on *The Tonight Show*, no matter who the host, the guests have to compete with the host in a "can you top this" type of environment to get laughs. But with me, it was possible to show one's human side.

And I also know that George realized that my size aided me in getting people to open up because I wasn't the least bit imposing. After his appearance he was talking to John Lollos while I was still on the set, standing on the Persian carpet that my chair was on, signing autographs, and George said: "You know why she's so good at what she does? She looks like if she fell off that carpet, she'd hurt herself."

It wasn't always easy to get big-name guests. Many were afraid that they would get blindsided by some personal question. Even after a publicity representative or agent would make the date, the preinterview phone call was often filled with the celebrity worrying about what was to be discussed. Of course, the longer the show ran, and the more word got out that being on the Dr. Ruth show—whatever version—was fun, and the easier it was to get celebrities.

Burt Reynolds was perhaps the biggest-name celebrity in my career as host and at that point it was a real coup. The production staff sent him baskets of fruits and flowers and other "bribes," but it was worth it, as it worked. What didn't work was the satellite. He was on as a live guest, but the satellite went out and so anyone looking to see the interview was disappointed. Of course, we taped the show, and it did get broadcast later on. But we'd gotten a lot of publicity that Burt was going to appear live on my show—and it was disappointing not to be able to take full advantage of it.

That happens to all of us. We build up a moment and when it arrives, either something goes wrong—or it just doesn't live up to our expectations. After the Burt Reynolds show, we went out to grab a bite to eat. Soon we were laughing and carrying on as much as usual. There would be more shows the following week; we couldn't allow our disappointment to spoil our joie de vivre. And you shouldn't be in your own home wearing a long face any more than I could on my television set. When something bad happens, complain as loudly as you can for five minutes and then put it aside. You've heard the phrase, "Get it out of your system." Well, I'm all for that. You're not permitted to allow small misfortunes to linger and fester—not if you want to have a life filled with joy.

Most people who don't know me think that I believe that nothing is sacred. But while I would talk about some aspects of a celebrity's personal life when they were on my shows—after all, they were experienced at being guests on TV shows, and every question was approved during the preinterview—I would never ask "real" people personal questions. When I had segments that involved people on the street revealing a sex problem to me that I would try to help them solve, the "guests" were actually actors pretending to have a particular problem. They had to memorize lines, though my answers weren't scripted. In this way we got the information out in an entertaining way, but without putting any regular people at risk.

It's my feeling that those who appear on a so-called reality TV show and spill all their dirty laundry are going to have their problems, whatever they might be, made even worse by telling all the world about it. My conscience won't allow me to do that, and it wasn't a part of my shows. I was once asked by *Good Morning America* to do a whole week's worth of segments and they wanted me to talk to viewers and try to help them with their sex problems. I suggested that they invest in a psychologist, whom the show would pay, to see these guests afterward to help them overcome the damage done by talking about their sex lives on national TV. That made my point, and *GMA* changed their mind about the segment.

On radio and on TV I spoke with real people on the phone, but their identities were hidden. Their family and friends would not know their private problems unless the client decided to make them aware of it. I am super careful about respecting the privacy of the people who come to me for therapy in my office. Now, if someone I speak to then goes around bragging to their friends that they spoke to me on the phone, that's up to them. I just won't shoulder the responsibility of making anyone else's life worse off to benefit my status.

When it comes to maintaining the joie de vivre in one's life, I advise others to maintain as much privacy as they can. If you spill the beans about your problems to friends and relatives, it might put added pressure on you, making the situation worse, not better. Of course, you might have a friend or relative who gives good commonsense advice and is always discreet; in that case, it's fine to discuss your problems. It can be a relief to unburden yourself. But choose that person carefully, because if you spill the beans to the wrong person, then your life could become more miserable. Keep in mind, telling your story to a professional counselor can be very helpful. Your friend may give you commonsense advice, but a professional has the training and experience to give you advice that has proved successful with other clients. That expertise is worth a lot. When I see a client and I know that I've helped lots of other clients with a similar problem, I can be fairly certain of meeting with success when advising this new client. But when your best friend gives you advice, it can be a hit-and-miss affair; following that advice might lead you even further down the wrong path.

Despite how much importance I place on maintaining people's privacy, things can sometimes go wrong. I had on as a guest Wayland Flowers, the ventriloquist, and his puppet, Madame. Madame is a bawdy lady, and the questions I was supposed to ask her were designed to elicit a certain kind of answer typical of her style. But before Wayland brought her out, I was to talk to him alone. The problem was that the questions I was supposed to ask Madame, which were sexual in nature, came up on the teleprompter when Wayland was out there without her—and I wound up asking him some very personal questions, ones I would never have dreamed of asking him without his guise of Madame. It took a moment or two for the right questions to be put on the teleprompter, so it was an awkward moment. But Wayland was a good sport and didn't complain.

I once had Lainie Kazan on as a guest. Before she came on stage, I'd taken some phone calls, and one was about oral sex. I'd told a woman who wanted to perform oral sex on her husband but wasn't sure of what to do, to practice on an ice cream cone. When Lainie came on, she had a follow-up question.

"Dr. Ruth, I heard you tell that woman to practice oral sex on an ice cream cone. That might be good advice for her, but what about we ladies who are always on a diet?"

"Lainie, then instead of putting ice cream in that cone," I answered her, "put low-fat frozen yogurt!"

The comedian David Brenner and I chatted about cuddling. I think it's very important, but David hated it.

"I don't like it when there are four arms in the bed. I have enough trouble figuring out where to put my two arms and then suddenly there's two more. Two minutes of cuddling is my maximum."

But I knew there must be more to this, and I got David to admit that when he was a boy he slept in the same bed as his brother. Now his dislike of cuddling made sense. He'd grown up wanting to have a bed of his own, and so even when he was sharing it with a woman with whom he was having sex, he still retained that dislike of sharing a bed.

What's important about a story like this isn't that we learned something about David Brenner but that anyone else viewing the segment who had a dislike of sharing their bed and who had been forced to do so as a child would realize the source of their problem. And even more important, their partner—who might be upset at being rejected and forced to sleep as far away as possible—would suddenly understand the underlying reason and so not take it personally.

Now, being a comedian, David talked about cuddling as if it were all a joke, but in fact we were discussing an issue that has serious ramifications among many couples. Small disagreements about an issue such as cuddling can lead to major problems. So while it may have seemed like this segment was just an excuse for David to be funny, in fact we may have saved some marriages out there among my viewing audience.

David's experiences as a child were having a negative effect on his joie de vivre as an adult. Sometimes you need the help of a therapist or even a psychiatrist to discover such issues, while sometimes all it takes is a little self-exploration. In David's case, knowing the source of the problem didn't change how he felt about sharing his bed, but as I said, knowing that source could definitely make a partner of his more understanding. So if you have issues like that, let your partner know where they stem from, assuming you do. I'm not saying you have to share them with the world, but with a lover it would be appropriate.

Let me add a caveat to what I just said. You need to be able to share much of your life with a partner, but you don't need to share all of it. Celebrities are surrounded by paparazzi, but you're not. If there are parts of your past that might undermine your relationship and haven't come out into the open, then my advice is to keep them under wraps. These could be negative parts of your life as well as positive ones. Here's an example of each type.

You're on a business trip; you go out to dinner with a coworker; you each have too much to drink and end up having sex, even though you're both married. You have no feelings for this person, you both regret what happened, and you promise yourself that you will never let this happen again. Do you tell your spouse? I say you don't. No matter how well your spouse takes this news, it's going to leave a scar on your relationship. You're not a celebrity, so there wasn't a reporter to see you and your coworker entering the elevator arm in arm, so your secret is safe. Better to leave it that way.

Your previous lover was well endowed, while your current partner is perhaps a little on the small side. Does it bother you when making love? He's a very good lover who always gives you orgasms, so the answer is no. If he asks you about your former partner in this department, my advice would be to tell a white lie and not report the size of his penis. It doesn't gain you anything but it could leave your current partner feeling badly and therefore take some of the joie de vivre out of each future time you have sex. As long as whatever it is you're hiding has almost no chance of leaking out, then this sort of cover-up is perfectly all right.

∾

Not every show was meant to be funny. I had as a guest Dr. Mathilde Krim, who at the time was leading the fight against AIDS. When I first started on radio, AIDS hadn't been discovered yet. Everyone was afraid of herpes, but while not a pleasant disease, herpes isn't deadly (except that the lesions caused by herpes may serve as entry points for the HIV virus to enter the body). But when I had my TV shows, AIDS was a sexually transmitted disease that was killing many, many people. At first it was mostly gay men, but it was obvious that that was the tip of the iceberg, and it was vital that the public be educated about the dangers of unprotected sex. Now, perhaps my ratings weren't as high when I tackled a subject such as AIDS but to me that didn't matter. What counts is that perhaps I saved a few people's lives by getting them to take precautions that they otherwise might not have.

Richard Simmons was someone I'd had on as a guest several times. As you know, he gives off a lot of energy when he's on TV, and he starts getting himself prepared the moment he walks into the building. He's constantly jumping around, screaming things at the top of his lungs, and just giving off as much energy as possible every second he's there.

Richard is usually promoting something, and on one occasion John said to him not to promote some health bar because he'd done it on his last appearance. Richard swore up and down that he wouldn't—but the moment he was in front of the cameras, he pulled the bar out from his gym shorts and started his spiel. All I could do was laugh, because you know what? I do the same thing.

When you're a guest on a show, it's often because you want to plug something. With me, it's often a new book, but it could be a show or an appearance. In any case, what is supposed to happen is that the host will ask you a question at one point that prompts your response about what it is you're plugging. However, what often happens with me is that we start talking about sex, the host gets very intrigued, and also knows that it makes for good ratings. The next thing you know, my five minutes are up and I never got to mention what I was there to plug. Having had that happen to me a number of times, I no longer wait for the host to ask me the question. As soon as I'm out there, I mention the book or whatever. I don't know if I learned that from Richard Simmons or not, but if you are ever on TV promoting something, all I can tell you is not to rely on the host, no matter how emphatic the producer is to trust that your product, book, or show will get the plug you seek. You have to take charge because you're not getting paid to be on the show, your compensation is the plug, so you better make certain that you get it.

I was often offered opportunities to go on other shows. Once I was asked to cohost the show *Friday Night Videos*. I had to think long and hard about that one because of who I was supposed to cohost with, Ozzy Osbourne. Of course, I didn't know who he was, but I did my homework, and when I read about some of the antics he'd done onstage—biting off the head of a chicken, for example—I wasn't so keen on the idea of sharing a stage with him! Maybe he'd bite off my head! But I was assured that he'd behave himself, and so I agreed.

Ozzy and I were put onto a set made to resemble a psychiatrist's office. I was sitting in a chair and he sat on a psychiatrist's couch, with his legs crossed under him. He wore a suit and, apart from his long hair, didn't look very scary. In fact, he was probably more afraid of what I might ask him than I was of what he might do. He turned out to be very civilized, but he did say that his "friends" had been asking him what Dr. Ruth's sex life was like, which was his round-about way of posing the question of me. Not only don't I ask personal questions, but I don't answer them either. But I do have sort of a standard answer for that one.

"Ozzy, I never allow my husband Fred to come to television appearances like this one. You know why?"

"Haven't got a clue, Dr. Ruth."

"Because you would ask him about our sex life and he would say, 'Don't listen to her, it's all talk!'"

The one show that I really loved being on was *Lifestyles of the Rich and Famous* because, thanks to Robin Leach and his producers, I got to see parts of the world that I otherwise might never have visited. They sent me, all expenses paid, to Africa, India, and China. And if I was sleeping in a tent in Africa, it was the most luxurious tent you could find. But to me, more important than the luxury accommodations—which I understood the viewers at home liked to see—was the fact that a production team took charge of making all the arrangements. All I had to do was show up and allow myself to be filmed in exchange for some fabulous trips that didn't cost me a cent. (If you hear any celebrities complaining about how hard it is to be one, cross them off your list of favorites!)

The One That Got Away

I was friends with Raymond Burr, better known to TV audiences as Perry Mason. He lived in California, where he had a house with a vineyard, but he would come to New York regularly, and we'd get together. One day he called me on a snowy day and said I had to come to lunch. I try not to venture out in New York when it snows because I live all the way uptown and the streets where I live are hilly, so I'm a bit afraid of not being able to get back home. But Raymond insisted, and we met at a fancy fish restaurant.

Raymond did the ordering—which I didn't mind, because when I'm at a restaurant with someone, I'm more interested in the conversation than the food. We were four at the table and I didn't hear what he told the waiter, but soon enough a five-tier platter loaded with assorted raw shellfish was set down in front of us, along with a magnum of wine, and all I was going to drink was one sip. More food followed, and most of it wound up on Raymond's plate. But while he was eating and drinking, he was also making me an offer.

"Ruth, I've got a great idea for a TV series for you."

"Raymond, quick, tell me. I'm all ears."

"I want you to be a tugboat captain. We'll shoot it up around Vancouver, where production costs are less. It'll be a big hit."

"A tugboat captain? Why do you think I would make a good tugboat captain?" I asked. That was a role I certainly never would have considered myself ideally suited for.

"I was given the script and it's a great part. It needs a lot of energy—that you have; a lot of chutzpah—which you have in spades; and I'll make sure there's a love interest for you."

I wasn't very confident about the premise and I'm not much of a sailor, so a TV show that would have me on a boat for long periods of time wasn't that appealing. But Raymond knew me well enough to have found my weak spot: a love interest.

Raymond put a lot of effort into trying to make this show a reality, but sadly he got sick and that slowed him down. When he passed away, that was the end of the project. One of the saddest parts—to me, at least—of his final days was that somehow the paparazzi had found out that he was sick and were following him to see if they could catch him going to the doctor, and he was doing all he could to maintain his privacy. That he would have to play such games during his last days made me very sad. So you see, sometimes you should be glad you're not a celebrity (though, as I said, you are the star of your own life and you should never forget that).

I love being on television because I know that I can spread my messages to a wide audience. And I watch some television, though not a lot. According to studies, the average American watches more than five hours of TV a day. To me, that's the best way to kill the joie de vivre in your life. Television sometimes entertains, and sometimes is educational, but it's a basically passive occupation. Oh, yes, you might guess along with the contestants on a game show, and if you watch an interview by Charlie Rose, you might learn something. But for the most part, you're existing while in front of the set, not really living and growing as a person. So my advice is not to use TV as a crutch. If there's something you really want to watch, go ahead, but don't just turn on the set because you're bored and need a companion. Your TV is not your best friend, and the less time you hang with it, the greater the potential for joie de vivre in your life.

CHAPTER VIII

Always Learn New Things

Since I'm known as Dr. Ruth, you can presume I have a doctorate. Mine is an EdD from Columbia University's Teachers College. Working backward, I also have a master's in sociology from the New School for Social Research. Go back a bit further and you'll discover that I have a . . . college degree? Not really; I studied psychology at the Sorbonne for four years, but I never got an actual degree before I left the country. A high school diploma? Nope, I have that utterly fabulous degree in Swiss housekeeping. And go all the way back to elementary school and the cupboard is completely bare. That's what growing up during wartime will do for your collection of diplomas. (By the way, I didn't just waltz into the New School without a degree. They had me take a couple of extra courses so that I qualified for graduate school.)

Because I was cheated by fate is why I put more value into education than some people. But it also means I appreciate that education doesn't necessarily have to be of the formal variety. There are many ways to expand your brain, and one of the best I've found is teaching.

I love to teach and have always done so, beginning as a kindergarten teacher in Israel and France all the way up to teaching graduates students as I do today. But some of the highlights of my teaching years didn't happen until a stage in my life when most people would have long given up standing in front of a classroom full of students. I taught at various colleges in the New York area over the years, but starting in 2003 at the age of seventy-five, I moved into the Ivy Leagues—first at Princeton and then Yale, and for a while I was actually teaching at both at the same time. You should have seen my limo bills!

In most areas I'm not a snob. I love what Nate Berkus did to my apartment (more on that in the next chapter), but bear in mind that I never moved from Washington Heights down to a ritzy part of Manhattan. I like nice clothes, but I wear them over and over. I eat at fancy restaurants but also at street-corner hot dog carts. You get the picture. However, when it comes to educational institutions, I admit I'm impressed by the Ivies. And so that Ruth K. Westheimer, who doesn't have a high school diploma, would be teaching at two of them at the same time was quite an ego boost. It actually made me feel at least an inch taller!

You know the expression, "Those who can, do; those who can't, teach"? Nonsense. To me, teaching is about learning, which takes a lot of doing. If you don't know your subject , your students will make sure you go home at the end of the day feeling rather downtrodden. And since I want to be admired by my students, I work hard to make sure that my classes have something of value.

The reason I like to teach at the age of eighty-six is that when you reach a certain stage, hanging around people your own age doesn't offer all that much in terms of growth potential. Many seniors have their sights aimed inward rather than outward. In part that's because they're trying to see which parts of their body are falling apart, so they become focused on their gall bladder or their knee rather than the world around them. And some don't see much of a future for themselves, so they don't really care to broaden their horizons. I'm just the opposite. To me, the broader my horizons, the more places I can hide out in order to elude Father Time. So I'd rather be in a room full of fresh young faces than one in which wrinkles predominate. And the brighter the brains behind those faces, the more I wind up learning from them.

And talk about joie de vivre! In my classrooms, it's the order of the day. I don't allow any electronics. I want everyone paying attention to me, not some screen. And everybody participates. You can't have good sex and be a bystander, and you can't learn that way either.

But this book is as much about you as it is about me—and you don't have to stand in front of an actual classroom to teach. If you have any young people in your family, make sure to pass on some words of wisdom. Just don't do it in a way that will bore them to death. Let's say you want to teach your granddaughter some of your favorite recipes. Force her to get her hands dirty. Talk about your family history as the meal you're making is in the oven. Make it lively and fun so she'll come back. And the more of your life you put into each lesson, the more fun you'll have as well.

∼

New Haven is not very far from New York City, but I took a rather circuitous route getting there. I had gone to a memorial for Yitzhak Rabin, the assassinated prime minister of Israel, at Madison Square Garden. At that event, one of the performances was by a young Israeli cellist, Inbal Megiddo, who all by herself, in front of tens of thousands of people, gave an extraordinary rendition of Joachim Stutschewsky's *Kaddish*. It was such a poignant moment in the event that afterward I made sure to seek her out to tell her how moved I was by her music. Inbal was studying at Yale, and she later contacted me to ask if I would speak at a Master's Tea at Calhoun College, one of the twelve residential colleges into which Yale is divided. It took so long to arrange for me to find the time to go up there that she'd actually graduated by the time the tea took place! But as far as I was concerned, the timing couldn't have been better.

Pierre drove me up on a gorgeous spring day. Most of the students were hanging out on the lawns, throwing Frisbees and enjoying the sunshine. At Calhoun I met the master, William Sledge, and his wife, Elizabeth. The large library in which I spoke was packed with students who greeted me enthusiastically and who posed very intelligent but frank questions afterward, such as, "How do you see the erosion of homophobia impacting heterosexual relationships?" and, "During intercourse, how does a male keep from hitting the cervix with his penis?" Questions such as these from very bright students challenge you, because you must give them an answer that meets the standard of the question.

We then moved to the dining hall, where the conversation with the students continued. Pierre and I sat with the Sledges. Bill is a psychiatrist, and he and Elizabeth had taken on the task of overseeing those Yalies living in the Calhoun residency hall. Bill—who has a long, distinguished list of credentials, including being the medical director of Yale–New Haven Psychiatric Hospital—is a southern gentleman who charms you with the combination of his slow drawl and quick, sharp intellect. I could see that he was seriously thinking about something, and by the time dessert had been served, he made his move.

"Dr. Ruth, your lecture this evening was a fine example of how to get our students to pay attention."

"My topic certainly helps keep their minds focused."

"Perhaps, but I know some professors who could give a lecture about sex that would make even the randiest young male in the auditorium turn his thoughts to his paper on anthropology."

"It says in the Talmud that a lesson taught with humor is one retained, and I always bear that in mind when I speak."

"Dr. Ruth, given your skill set, I wonder whether you would consider blessing this campus with your presence on a more regular basis."

"You mean teach a class?"

"That is exactly what I mean."

"You know that I'm already teaching a seminar at Princeton."

"While I respect my colleagues in New Jersey, I would argue that New Haven has just as much to offer you."

"I like your proposition, but let me make one of my own. Since I have a busy schedule, I could use some help in my classroom. Would you be willing to share the duties of this course, whatever it would turn out to be?"

"Dr. Ruth, sharing the lectern with you is not something that I had previously considered, but I'd be honored."

I ended up sharing the teaching duties of my Yale classes with Bill, but since Bill was equally busy with his hospital duties, we added a third member to our teaching troika, another Yale dean, Steve Lassonde, who has since become the dean of student life at Harvard. With this team in place, I had to lead, and therefore prepare, for only one lecture out of three. But I was always there to answer our students' questions at the end of class, which as you might guess usually had nothing to do with Jewish or American family life—the topic of our seminar as listed in the catalog—but instead the birds and the bees.

Later I taught a class on Sex and the Jewish Tradition with the Yale rabbi, James Ponet, the same class that I was teaching at Princeton on my own. But at both institutions, I didn't limit my education to what I could pick up from my students. I would make a day of it, attending other lectures or going to a concert or play in the evening. Here I was at universities where the students paid $50,000 a year to attend, in part because of these extracurricular activities, so I wasn't going to let them slip through my little fingers if I had the opportunity to share in them.

I can't cover the topic of my teaching years at Yale without mentioning the Beatle. Even though my title was only lecturer, I never failed to attend the graduation ceremonies. I love pomp and circumstance, and considering how much my Columbia cap and gown cost me when I graduated, I always try to amortize that cost whenever the opportunity presents itself.

In 2008, Yale honored Sir Paul McCartney with an honorary degree in music. I made sure to sit at the end of an aisle, and as Sir Paul was walking up toward the platform to receive his diploma, I stepped out from my seat and he spotted me.

"Dr. Ruth!" he cried out.

"Sing me something!" I shouted back.

So Sir Paul stopped the procession, came over to me, bent down, and sang "She loves you, yeah, yeah, yeah." An AP photographer happened to be nearby, and the picture of that moment circulated the globe. I felt a little guilty that I had stopped the entire graduation procession, but then again, it was one of those Westheimer maneuvers that I'll never forget!

Speaking of forgetting, you may have noticed when I led into this story I used the term "the Beatle." I have to be honest. I know very little about modern-day music, and while I'm well aware of the existence of the Beatles—how could anyone not—I still don't really know the names of the four of them. And so I wasn't excited to meet Paul McCartney in particular, but a Beatle. And to this day, I sometimes forget his name . . . but I always remember the story of the Beatle.

Most colleges that allow those not on the faculty to teach a course limit the number of semesters they're allowed to do so. I actually pushed the envelope at both Yale and Princeton to six years, but as they say, all good things must come to an end. Still, I haven't stopped teaching. I'm currently at my old alma mater, Columbia Teachers College, teaching a course on Family and Media; and as ever, my students are teaching me something during every class. But as I said, to me teaching doesn't necessarily have to be in front of a classroom. One other way that I've set about educating people, in numbers more than I could ever reach in a classroom, is by producing documentaries. But before I get to those, allow me to name-drop another famous institution of higher learning, Oxford.

I was invited to take part in one of their famous debates. Normally I don't like to debate because for the most part, the end result is that nobody changes their mind. But this was Oxford with a long history of notable debates, and so here was an opportunity that I couldn't pass up. The topic was abortion and sex education. While I wish there were no abortions, I am also strongly in favor of women retaining the right to control their bodies. However, it's a subject that stirs up a lot of emotions on both sides of the issue, not to mention on both sides of the Atlantic.

I don't like to lose, and it seems the fates didn't want me to lose this debate. The person leading the team against mine was a well-known Irish Catholic woman with strong views against abortion and sex education. By chance—or maybe by divine intervention—I happened to meet her sister in New York before flying off to England. These two sisters were on opposite ends of the political spectrum. When she learned that I would be debating her sister, she was not just willing to give me every possible edge, she was eager. We made a date at the Palm Court in the Plaza Hotel to have tea, and in that imposing room, as a harpist played in the background, she gave me all the dirt she could dish. But the most helpful piece of information she passed on was this: "My sister's a lush. She loves her glass of wine, and the second and the third as well. Given the circumstances, she'll make an effort to stay sober, but it won't be easy for her if there's a bottle of wine anywhere nearby." I didn't say a word at that, but smiled to myself. I'd heard all that I needed to know.

The Oxford Union is probably the premier debating society in the world. It remains separate from Oxford University, to maintain its freedom to debate any subject, including the controversial ones, but to me it spoke of the best of Britain's educational institutions. Entering the impressive Gothic-style building in which it is housed sent a shiver up my spine as I thought of all the illustrious people who had preceded me. Before the actual debate there is a dinner in the MacMillan Room that both teams attend. The dining hall is two stories high, with two tiers of windows and beamed ceilings. There was enough tableware in front of me to make me nervous that I'd pick up the wrong spoon or fork at some point during the meal. But also before me was the key to my ultimate victory, my wine glass.

As the dinner progressed, I made a point of proposing toast after toast. "To Oxford." "To the Queen." "To debating." Each time I raised my glass, but not a drop of wine passed my lips. My opponent, on the other hand, had to ask to have her glass filled several times. By the end of that dinner, the outcome of the debate was sealed.

One highlight of the debate, at least as I saw it, came when one of the members of the other side, a young man, spoke. "As a medical student I know my anatomy, but I'm not in need of sex ed because I'm a virgin and intend to stay that way until I am married." I suppose he thought I would attack or make fun of him for his status, as here again, those on the opposing side made the mistake of thinking of me as some sort of sexual deviant. "Young man," I said, "you are to be commended for saving yourself until marriage. As an observant Jew, I see nothing wrong with being a virgin and waiting until you are married to have sex. But just as you wouldn't want to take care of a patient without the proper training, I also believe that you shouldn't go to bed for the first time with your wife without also knowing exactly what to do to give her the most pleasure." Of course, the audience roared at that. One point for our side.

As for my main opponent, she was having trouble getting her thoughts straight. I'd seen videos of a few of her television appearances, and she had some very convincing arguments that she made eloquently. But I could tell the first time she opened her mouth that evening that the wine had had a considerable effect on her ability to think straight.

The audience decides which team has won, and the way they vote is similar to how they vote in the Houses of Parliament: they exit through either the "aye" or "nay" door. I watched carefully as the crowd left the room and the vast majority went through the door that favored my side of the debate. Another successful Westheimer maneuver!

Now, don't get me wrong, I have nothing against alcohol. I recommend a glass of wine or two to loosen inhibitions before having sex. I even came out with my own line of low-alcohol wine, Vin d'Amour. But too much alcohol will only mean that those imbibing will fall asleep rather than have terrific sex, and possibly wake up much worse for wear.

Far too many people seem to require alcohol or drugs in order to have a good time. That, to me, is very sad. I'm not saying that these substances don't offer any pleasurable aspects, but if they become requirements to feeling pleasure, then something is wrong.

I mentioned earlier that toddlers squealing with delight are the perfect example of joie de vivre. Well, toddlers aren't using recreational drugs, legal or otherwise, except maybe for mother's milk. At that age they can just let go of their feelings. If you need alcohol or drugs to let go or embrace your feelings of joy, then take that as a sign that something is wrong and see if you can't get it fixed. It could be something wrong with you or your relationship or something else altogether. Alcohol and drugs should just add a little lubrication. If they're being substituted as the entire experience of having fun, then that's not joie de vivre; it's fear of life.

Documentary Filmmaker

I didn't set out to be a sex therapist, yet I ended up doing fairly well in that field. Making documentaries wasn't something I ever had on my list of things to do either, but I've now done six, and though I don't have any planned right this minute, that could change as quickly as it took to make the decision to make the first one.

What set me off on this new tack was the last major exodus of Ethiopian Jews who were flown to Israel in May of 1991. As someone with a master's in sociology, I recognized that this was a singular moment in history taking place. These Ethiopians were going from a backward culture to becoming fully immersed in a very modern one. That would change them in a multitude of ways and over a very short period of time. This was an event that was unlikely ever to be repeated. The only reason that Israel accepted these immigrants was because they practiced a form of Judaism. No other large group of primitive people had such a bond with a modern counterpart, so this was a once-in-a-lifetime opportunity to study what would happen after they set foot in the twentieth century. And as soon as I realized that, I made up my mind to take on this challenge of documenting the absorption of the Ethiopian Jews into Israel.

Let me be very clear: I'm not a filmmaker. But if I set my mind to it, I can be a rainmaker. In other words, I have some talents in front of the camera, but zero behind one. My job as executive producer is to come up with the concept of the documentary, find someone who has the expertise to actually write a script and shoot the film, and then work some magic to come up with the money to complete the project. One reason that magic is required is that documentaries are not money-making propositions. They're not even break-even propositions. And if they get on national television—as many of mine have done—then that will cost even more money. So why does anyone bankroll these sinkholes? Maybe it's to see their names roll by quickly on the credits. I don't actually know, because I would never put any of my money into someone else's documentary. I'm not a rich person with money to burn, but I am someone who knows how to ask rich people to allow me to burn some of their money for one of my projects.

The documentary was titled *Surviving Salvation*, and for a filmmaker I linked up with Malcolm Clarke, who was an Oscar winner (and, by the way, won again in 2014). In addition to the documentary, which eventually aired on PBS, there was also an accompanying book that I coauthored with a professor from the Hebrew University, Steve Kaplan. And it's the book's cover that tells the story as well as anything.

On the cover there are two pictures of a family. In one, the elders are all in front, dressed in their traditional garb, with the young people in the back, as befits the society from which they came where elders are to be respected. (In fact, back home, the Beta Israel, as they were called, considered their first gray hairs as a source of pride, indicating that they were becoming of greater importance in their society.) Turn the book upside down and you see the second picture. In this one, taken only six months after the first, it's the young people in front, wearing blue jeans and sneakers, while the elders are relegated to the back, illustrating the dramatic transformation that took place among these people. The elders weren't able to fully adapt to their new surroundings, while the young people—though coming from the same backward villages—were much quicker to adjust, and so their societal norms were turned upside down. The elders, instead of retaining command, had to rely on the young to lead the way.

But the role reversals in the two societies go far deeper than just age. In Ethiopian society, men are "first" and given more respect. A woman is always to defer to a man. When these Ethiopian people came to Israel, they were suddenly confronted with social workers, almost all of whom were female. How to react? The social worker was in a position of authority, able to decide the man's fate as far as where he and his family would live, and so on, yet his upbringing led him to believe that she should listen to him.

I ran into similar situations when doing the documentary. Here I was, a woman, asking questions (through an interpreter, of course) of these Beta Israel men. If I'd been a woman back in Ethiopia, they would have refused to listen to me; but in Israel, they weren't quite sure how to react. And this was especially so because I was invading their space, so to speak, by asking them personal questions. There was one gentleman, perhaps forty years old—thus making him an elder—dressed in his traditional garb, which included a flowing robe and a scarf wrapped around his head. And there I was, dressed in a skirt (as I knew the slacks I would normally have been wearing would not have been deemed appropriate) and a short-sleeve shirt, as the temperature was in the nineties.

"How are you adjusting to life in Israel?" I asked him. To me, as a sociologist, this was an innocent question. But in part because I was a woman, he was loath to offer any criticisms, as that would have been a sign of weakness when speaking to this woman, even further down the totem pole because of her size. He looked down at me for a moment, considered where this question was coming from, and said, "Thank you." It wasn't that he didn't understand the question, but rather he didn't really want to give an honest answer to someone like me, so he preferred to dodge it.

However, when I'd lived in Israel many years before, one of my jobs had been as a teacher of Yemenite children, another group of immigrants. Dealing with children is always easy, but I'd had to learn to deal with their parents—who, like this Ethiopian man, didn't quite trust me. The key to getting your message across is patience. Now, I am an impatient person, so it took me quite some time to absorb that lesson. Once I did, though, I never lost the knack. So in this case, I answered him in kind. "Thank you," I said, and then, very firmly, "How are you adjusting to life in your new land?"

He could sense that I wasn't about to go away. Slowly he told me of some of the difficulties that he was having, such as living in a very small apartment several stories in the air, a condition that he, as a goat herder who was used to always being connected directly to the land, found disconcerting. Our discussion lasted quite some time. I teased more and more information from him as he began to consider me not as a female but as someone who possessed some authority and should be respected. In fact, that is how the Ethiopian men learned to treat all the women in authority that they met. They were able to "desexualize" them, creating a new category in their minds.

In addition to this documentary on the Beta Israel, I've also done one about the Druze in Israel, the Bedouins in Israel, and the Circassians in Israel. Notice a pattern? There are a couple of reasons for this choice of locale. You want good weather when you make a documentary on a shoestring and can't afford rain dates, and during the summer months in Israel you're as likely to have your shoot rained out as me to slam-dunk a basketball. You can also hire a crew for a much more reasonable price. But most of all, it means that your producer gets to spend several weeks in the land she loves, driven by some gentlemen who'll do pretty much anything she asks.

But while Israel may be a prime shooting locale for practical reasons, the actual theme of my documentaries is always linked to the family. Since I lost mine, I very much appreciate the importance of family and so want to show the world via these films how different people manage their family lives. For *The Olive and the Tree*, a film about the Druze, the main question was how these people maintain their identity while living in a country where they are a teeny minority. For *Shifting Sands*, I wanted to show how Bedouin women are advancing and how that affects their society.

Traditionally, a Bedouin woman could never meet with a man by herself. She actually risked death in doing so. For me to speak with Bedouin men was problematic, though it was always in a group—even an "old" woman such as I couldn't be left alone with a Bedouin man. The setting was also uncomfortable because the Bedouin are uncomfortable in the housing that is forced upon them by the State of Israel. The older generation looks back with yearning on their former nomadic life, and to be sitting in a house sharing a cup of coffee, rather than sitting on pillows outside a tent, is not what they want from life.

Hussein a-Rafayah wore the traditional headdress, and his skin was olive brown. He served me coffee, but not in the same way that he would serve a man. I would get one full cup and that's that. As a woman, it's all I was worthy of. A man would get a smaller first serving but then several more. Actually, as many as he wanted. Everything the Bedouins do follow the ancient traditions, at least for those of the older generations.

I asked Hussien if he isn't better off now than before. He looked at me with sad eyes and before replying gave a heavy sigh, expressing to me before his words came out that I would never understand what it meant to be a Bedouin. "You look at this room and you say to yourself, 'Here is a modern Bedouin, a happy Bedouin, content with modern life and its comforts.' Wrong. I am not a happy Bedouin. I have not adjusted because I did not choose this life. I feel imprisoned in my own home. I still miss the nomadic life in the desert. I dream of the day I wake up in the land of my grandparents, without books and running water, without a brick shelter over my head—but as a free person."

❧

He was certainly right about one thing: I never want to live in a tent in the middle of the desert. And I say that not as conjecture but from experience, because actually, I *did* live in a tent for a time when I first arrived in Israel, which back then was more desert than anything else, and lived on a kibbutz. I wasn't even alone in that tent. I shared it with two men. Had I been a Bedouin, my family would have pinned a target on my back for such living arrangements. But I didn't have a family to rely on for company, so sharing a tent with two men wasn't such a terrible experiment. However, while I tolerated living in that tent, it's not a habitat I want to make a return to anytime soon, though my escape route was actually not all that bad. You see, if you became paired with someone from the opposite sex (and no, it wasn't one of my tent mates), the kibbutz moved you from a tent into an actual building with four walls and a roof. Israel needed babies, so any inducement to baby making—for example, some privacy—was yours for the asking. I'm not saying that I found a boyfriend on the kibbutz solely because that allowed me to give up tent living, but I also won't tell you that before I met that guy the thought had never crossed my mind. What these stories illustrate is that when we look at the situation in the Middle East today, without understanding that someone might prefer a tent, we can't possibly understand the dynamics of the area. And while book learning is wonderful, it doesn't compare to going out into the real world and examining life on the ground as it is taking place.

～

Another group of Muslims living in Israel that attracted my attention were the Circassians. Their land is part of Russia now, as the entire native population was forcibly evicted by the czar in 1864. While most Circassians live in Turkey, there are small pockets of them here and there—including, of all places, Wayne, New Jersey. But it was the village of Kfar Kama in Israel that I visited with my film crew.

One aspect of Circassian culture that made me want to learn more about them is their marriage customs. In truth, today only some ritual enactments of the old ways remain. But the way a Circassian male would finalize the choice of his bride was to ride up to where she lived on horseback, grab her, and carry her away to his clan. This kidnapping was usually not unexpected, as a relationship would have been brewing and the young woman in question was perfectly safe. The women of the family of the man who'd abducted her would make sure that once he deposited her in their midst, that he would have no further contact with her. Circassians are Muslims and obey the rules of that religion. The abduction was just the opening salvo in negotiations between the family of the abductor and that of the young woman. But Circassian traditions say that while the parents may object, they can't stop a couple from marrying, so sometimes these abductions were a bit more than ceremonial—though once they occurred, the two families would settle matters peaceably and the arrangements for the marriage would be made.

Like the Bedouins, the Circassians would prefer nothing more than to return to their homeland but for the time being that's not possible and may never be. However unlike the Bedouins, the Circassians have adapted themselves to their new homelands, and in Israel they speak Hebrew as well as the Israelis, and the men serve in the armed forces. But this yearning for "home" never leaves them. I interviewed Adnan Gerkhad, a seventy-year-old retired school principal. To look at him, you would see nothing much different than any other Israeli. If his skin seems a little dark, that comes not from his background, as Circassians can be fair, but his hourlong daily morning hike in the sun to stay in shape. He wears a green shirt, khaki slacks, and sandals—again, nothing at all unusual for an Israeli man. We are at a café in the Circassian village of Kfar Kama, but this café could be in any Israeli town; there is nothing to distinguish Kfar Kama to make it appear particularly Circassian. In part that's because while almost every Circassian can speak their native tongue,

Adyghe, few can write it. And so the menus are written in Hebrew as are the signs on the wall advertising Coca-Cola and Fanta. Circassian children are taught to speak in Adyghe, but once they enter the school system, they are taught to speak, read, and write in Hebrew so that those Circassians who have grown up in Israel speak it perfectly, and that's the language Adnam and I used to converse.

"What are the difficulties of maintaining your culture?" I asked him.

"We face many difficulties in keeping our culture alive. Obviously there is the Israeli culture that surrounds us everywhere. We are like a small boat sailing in the great ocean of Israel. But while there is a strong Arab culture here, it is not our culture. Yes, we are Muslims, but we are not Arabs. Our children learn Arabic in order to study the Koran, but Circassian society has a much different culture than that of the Arabs."

"Before I came here to film this documentary, I met with some Circassians in the New York area," I told him. It was part of my preliminary research. "Certainly it is no easier for them than had they lived here."

"In Turkey there are many Circassians. It is easier to maintain our traditions when you have a larger population. I'm sure the Circassians in America have similar problems to those of us here in Israel. On the one hand, American culture is so overwhelming—just look around you and you'll see so many signs of American influence. That must be hard to combat, I'm sure. But in America, it is a melting pot, and nobody really cares what you are. And yes, gradually you become assimilated, but you can also hold on to your values. Israel is Jewish and we are Muslim. Assimilation is not really possible, and that means there is a jagged edge between our two cultures. We are accepted and yet we are not."

If there is anyone who can understand the feelings he expressed that morning, it's me. When I was sixteen and the war ended, I too was at sea. I felt German, but as a Jew I could not go back to Frankfurt and all the terrible memories that lay around every corner. So my tradition as a German Jew had been yanked out from under me, along with everything else. I went to Palestine, soon to be Israel, but it never felt like I was going home. When I moved to Paris, I loved the city, but it wasn't *my* city. New York is now my city, and I am at home there. Yet there will always be a part of me that longs for that original home, just like the Circassians long for their homeland. So while ostensibly I'm making a study of the Druze or the Bedouin or the Circassians, in actuality part of my reason for making these documentaries is that I'm looking for what I lost in 1938. And if the transition the Ethiopian Jews had to make was much broader than mine, at least they came as whole villages, family members, and neighbors. When the ship I was on landed in Palestine, I was jumping off into a new world by myself while still a teenager. No easy task, I can assure you. Especially as the British decided to put all of us on that boat in a camp behind barbed wire, just like the pictures I'd seen of concentration camps. Our group from Heiden had the proper papers, but rather than separate us out from those arriving illegally, we were all lumped together for a week. Let me tell you, this was quite a shock. We'd been singing and dancing on the boat all night waiting to get our first glimpse of Palestine, and then we found ourselves behind barbed wire. Luckily I was with friends, and after a week, we were sent off to the kibbutzim to which we'd been assigned.

◆

Maintaining culture requires other people from that culture. It's not something you can do alone or you would quickly drown. But building your knowledge base doesn't require anyone else, other than some good teachers. And as I said, learning doesn't require a formal setting, and one of my favorite informal settings is what are known as Renaissance Weekends. Started by Linda and Philip Lader some thirty years ago, Renaissance Weekends are retreats geared toward bringing together a variety of different people from different fields—government, science, media, sports, the arts—who congregate to discuss a wide variety of topics. Everyone who attends is required to participate, so while you can just sit in on some discussions, you must lead others. Bill and Hillary Clinton were early attendees, though once Bill became president they had to end their participation. But I've met Supreme Court justices, one of whom I always make sure to dance with, and a host of other people. It's a family affair, and I always lead one seminar for the teens on sex.

Nobody stands on ceremony, and everyone wears a name tag. Or almost everyone. Though there are half a dozen of these weekends scattered throughout the year, I only go to the one at New Year's held in Charleston, South Carolina. I've mentioned already several times that though I may be a part of US pop culture, I'm not all that familiar with the other club members. So I was at a reception at Renaissance when a woman came up and started speaking to me, saying how much she admired me—but she wasn't wearing a name tag. I will admit that I was probably the only person there who would not have instantly recognized Barbra Streisand, but I didn't. Maybe I'm bad at recognizing famous faces because I'm always looking up at everyone and when you see their pictures in the papers, the angle is straight on. In any case, I said to Barbra, "And what do you do?" I could tell that she was annoyed that I didn't recognize her, but *c'est la vie*.

Renaissance fits my ideal learning situation because while there is so much new information and insight to absorb every minute of the day, everyone also has the duty to pass on something about what they are experts in. And we're at a hotel, not a school. Over the years, many of us become fast friends, so the social connectivity adds to the overall ambiance.

Another way that I teach is by answering people's questions, either in my syndicated newspaper column or online. On the one hand, it's harder to learn from this form of teaching because the questions are very similar. A number of years ago, BookExpo America, the book convention, was in Chicago where *Playboy* had its headquarters, and since I'm friends with Hugh and Christie Hefner, I was naturally invited to a party they threw for convention goers. With the name *Playboy* attached to the invitation, lots of people wanted to be there, hoping to see a Bunny or two, so the lounge high up in the building was filled. Since I don't drink very much alcohol—in fact, none at such parties—I was circulating with my glass of soda when a man stopped me.

"Dr. Ruth, so glad to meet you. I write the *Playboy* "Advisor" column."

He was relatively young, dressed conservatively in a sports jacket and slacks, and he might have been your average college professor, though he—like me—made a living out of answering people's questions about sex.

"You've been doing this for years," he said, "but I only recently replaced the old columnist and I have to ask you a question. How do you keep doing this week after week when really there are only ten questions that people ask?"

To some extent, what he said was very true. Most of the questions I get are about premature ejaculation or women with difficulties reaching orgasm. It's so very rare to get a question that surprises me, though it happens. You might think since I and other advice givers, like the gentleman at *Playboy*, have answered these questions over and over that everyone would know the answers and stop asking them. There are a number of reasons why that's not true—one of them being that young people who begin having sex start out relatively clueless, and so there is a steady influx of new people looking for this information. And then you may know nothing about plumbing until your toilet backs up on a Sunday evening and you can't get a plumber. Similarly, as long as someone's sex life seems to be working OK, they don't bother learning the finer points. But as soon as they run into a problem, since they're embarrassed to ask anyone else, they'll turn to someone like me.

But the other reason that the public likes reading material such as this is that although the underlying problems may be similar, the stories that people offer are quite different. So while my answers may be similar and educational, the questions themselves are different and rather gossipy. And you know what—even I enjoy reading many of these in order to peek into other people's lives. Because sex is almost always done in private, none of us know what is going on in other people's bedrooms, and because of that hidden nature of sexual activity, we are all curious about it, even me, despite having answered so many questions either in my office or in the media. And I learn from these questions too, because different scenarios offer new insights into how people's minds work and what is happening out there. For example, someone wrote in saying she is a professional GFE courtesan. Sorry—I didn't know what that was when I received the letter, but I do now: a woman who pretends to be your girlfriend in bed rather than one who is just a prostitute.

By the way, this professional GFE had become bored with sex. I wish I could have offered her a cure, but I'm afraid that if you're having sex all day long with strangers, it's going to affect your personal sex life, no doubt about it.

One reason I'm sure this woman was bored with sex is that she told me that when she's with a client, she fakes her reaction, possibly not finding any of it pleasurable, no matter how loudly she groans with pleasure. A woman can derive a lot of pleasure from sex even if she doesn't have an orgasm, and putting pressure on herself, or having pressure put on her by her partner, to have an orgasm each and every time she has sex is going to reduce her joie de vivre.

Obviously, I counseled the woman carefully, but I also felt there was an interesting experiment to pass on from that story. Why not try making love and not allowing oneself to go all the way. It would be similar to the experience that wine tasters have. They taste the wine and then spit it out so that they don't consume too much alcohol. When they're not tasting, they drink wine like everybody else and appreciate both the taste and the effects of the alcohol, but I'm sure that they would all tell you that just tasting is a satisfying experience.

Why try this? Because if you're always waiting for that orgasm, you won't enjoy the rest of the lovemaking as much. You risk being goal oriented, impatiently waiting for that orgasm. But if you tell yourself ahead of time that you're not going to have an orgasm and instead will try to enjoy everything else to make up for it, I bet you'll see the rest of what lovemaking can offer in a different light. And that pleasure will help you increase your joie de vivre.

But really, I've heard it all! There was the woman whose husband would go to Goodwill to obtain used women's panties in order to masturbate into them, and she was jealous of these other women. And the woman who complained that her vagina didn't smell! Sometimes I laugh at these questions when I read them, but I always answer them seriously, because the people who are writing in are serious—and I also know that there are other people out there with similar problems who are looking for real answers.

What do I learn from such questions? When you can honestly say, "I've heard it all," it makes it much easier to do your job as a therapist. When an individual or couple comes to me for help with a problem, I can't look surprised, even if I am. But I also can't look bored. I need to have a fairly neutral expression, at least until I know the people sitting with me a little better. They're expecting professional behavior on my part and that's exactly what I want to provide. Now, most of the time the problems are of the so-called garden variety that I've seen hundreds of times. But when the problem is a little unusual, having this memory bank full of odd questions helps me maintain a straight face.

No matter how much training a therapist has, he or she also needs a certain amount of creativity. If a therapist is giving the exact same ten answers over and over again, boredom will set in, and you can't be an effective therapist while yawning because you're hearing the same story for the hundredth time. So answering unusual questions keeps me on my toes and helps me hone my skills.

Let me end this chapter with another question I was asked on radio. A young man called and said he was soon to be married. I congratulated him and asked him what his question was. "Dr. Ruth, we're not virgins, and I want to find a way to make our first time having sex as newlyweds special. Do you have any suggestions?" I thought about it for a split second, which is all the time I had because when you're on radio, the most important rule is not to allow any dead air (that's to say, silence). Luckily I can think fast on my feet, and so I said to him, "When you come out of the bathroom, I want you to wear nothing else but a tie and a top hat." He responded, "And where do I put the hat?"

CHAPTER IX

Take Risks

I may be only four foot seven, but I think what you've read about my life proves that I'm tougher than my size indicates. Life has thrown some rather tough punches my way, yet I've managed to succeed beyond my wildest dreams, literally. When I was in Heiden, they used to show us movies once in a while, and the ones I loved best were those starring Shirley Temple. She was so cute, so talented; most of all, though, watching her sing and dance helped all of us forget where we were and raised our spirits, at least while the movie projector was turning. You couldn't stare up at the screen and see one of her movies without feeling there was hope in the world, even living in an orphanage. And since as a little girl she was short and I was short, well, that made me love her all the more. But to imagine that I might one day be even a little bit famous was so unrealistic that such thoughts never entered my mind. In America, where, as they say, anyone can grow up to be president, boys dream of following in the footsteps of their sports heroes and girls dream of becoming a ballerina. But when you're an orphan in a war, your dreams are much more modest. Did I fantasize about seeing my parents? All the time. But becoming a celebrity like Shirley Temple was unimaginable.

For a child of ten to have gone through what I did could have left me traumatized. When I'd finally reached a certain level of safety, I could have parroted Voltaire in *Candide* and said, "Let me tend to my little garden." I wouldn't criticize anyone who goes through traumatic events such as I did for pulling back rather than taking risks. But if there's one thing I'm not it is laid back, which is why I could never live in a place where the operative word is *"mañana,"* since my philosophy calls for everything right this very second! Not only did I bounce back, I ended up bouncing higher and higher. I didn't allow myself to be cowed by the world; instead I was always willing to take on new challenges. Like a turtle, a creature that is meaningful to me for this very reason, I'm willing to stick my neck out and take risks. The trial balloon I floated in front of those managers of community affairs at radio stations was one risk I took that perhaps had the biggest payoff, but it wasn't the only one.

The Road to Television

Fred Silverman had been the head of both ABC and NBC, and his track record of discovering hit shows was extensive. So when he approached me about doing a television show, I had to take it seriously. I know I'm famous for saying that size doesn't matter, but that's in the bedroom. In business, I think size—and by that I'm referring to a person's track record, not their height or the size of their sexual equipment—is very important. Yet while I had a hit radio show, I still thought of myself as a college professor. That I still am teaching at college at the age of eighty-six proves that it's the career goal for which I still have the most affinity. And while my notoriety on radio might have made some academic department heads shy away from me, radio wasn't toxic to a career in education. But a television show was another matter. If I stepped in front of those cameras as the host rather than as a guest, I was certain I would say good-bye to academia. Which explains why when Fred called, I felt a little like Eve in front of that apple tree. The lure of the apple was great, but I wasn't so sure that I wanted to feel that naked either.

In the end, the deciding factor for me was that television would allow me to reach a bigger audience. I believed strongly that as a sex educator, I had important information to spread to the world. I'm not claiming to have done the research, and my passion wasn't in poring over data, but I am very passionate about telling the world about the findings of researchers in my field. And while I could do a more thorough job in a classroom over the course of a semester, I could certainly reach a lot more people by going on television. So I agreed.

We shot what is called a pilot, a concept I really don't like because it's too much like a first date. Just because one spills wine on a companion's lap on the first date doesn't mean that the relationship is doomed. But in television, you get it right the first time or you're out. I think very highly of Fred, but I do have to wonder about his choice of the cohost he chose for me. Here I was a TV newbie, and he chose another radio person who had even less TV experience than I did—at least I'd been a guest on dozens of shows. In any case, we filmed the pilot at the studios of Channel 5 in New York, but despite Fred's long list of credentials (or maybe because of it), the cost was too high, and he couldn't get enough stations interested. It didn't survive the pilot stage.

Did I let that stop me? I know I said I was hesitant to do a TV show, but once I was committed to the idea, I hated the thought of failing. So I walked into the office of the general manager of Channel 5, Bob O'Connor, who I knew had wanted to air the show.

"Bob, Fred just told me that he couldn't get enough stations and so he's pulling the plug."

"Yes, he called to tell me. Sorry, Ruth. I think it could have done quite well in this market."

"Don't be sorry—let's do it anyway. Fred said the problem was that the show cost too much money to produce but we could do a local version for a lot less money."

"You'd be willing to do it for less?" he asked incredulously. Bob wasn't used to the people in front of the cameras willing to take a reduction in salary.

"If the show is a success, we both know I'll be compensated. But if it never gets on the air, I won't make a dime, so absolutely, make me an offer and the answer is yes."

They gave me a time slot on weekday mornings. I took phone calls like I did on radio, but I also interviewed celebrities and experts, and I interacted with the people in the studio audience. We were doing well in the ratings, and they moved us to another time slot, bumping another show which hadn't been doing too well.

Television series get approved in batches—usually either twenty-six for a full season or thirteen for half a season. At the end of our first thirteen-week run, I was told that we were renewed for another thirteen weeks. When there's good news, I want to celebrate, so we had a party and I danced the night away. Then two days later I was called into a meeting. I thought it was to discuss the new season. But when I saw the faces on the men in that office and they told me to sit down, I knew what was coming, though I didn't find out why for a couple of years.

It turns out that the owner of the station was a devout Catholic and when he went to arrange to have his new baby baptized, he was told that for that to happen in church, he had to take that doctor who said it was OK to have an abortion off the air. He didn't really care about my show so given that alternative, he gave the order to cancel. And I didn't dance that night.

I don't regret for a minute those thirteen shows that I did. It gave me the experience so that when the next opportunity came along, I was ready for it. You can't be a risk taker and expect to win each and every time. If you could control the future, then you wouldn't be taking any risks. And while failure leaves a bitter taste in your mouth, the sweetness of winning more than makes up for it, and you'll never win at anything unless you take a risk in the first place. As I've said a number of times, joie de vivre requires the ability to take the good and the bad. Life is much more like a roller coaster than a calm stream, but those who ride roller coasters often end up going back again and again because the thrills are what make life worth living.

Fred Silverman had taken a risk with me, and he did it again a number of years later. Pierre thought up the idea of a sitcom that I could star in. The basic premise was that I would be a college professor (you know I liked that portion of the idea right from the start!) and that I lived in a big house where I rented rooms to a bunch of students. He wrote the script for a pilot, which I took to Fred. Fred liked it and knew a production company that had a deal with ABC to do a pilot. They liked our premise—and Pierre and I were off to Hollywood.

I was experienced with talk shows. Not only had I been on so many others, but by that time I had hosted hundreds of my own. But sitcoms are a different animal. I was of course familiar with the genre. Fred Westheimer was addicted to *The Odd Couple*. He watched every episode anew and in reruns, over and over. I never spent that much time in front of the TV, but I'd certainly seen many hours of that show; since they're all constructed from a similar formula, I had a basic understanding of what the finished product was like. What I didn't know was how they get to that finished product in Hollywood.

Pierre and I were introduced to Allan Leicht, the head writer and the other writers. They'd all driven up in Ferraris and other fancy cars as sitcom writers get paid handsomely. Of course, in Hollywood the word "writer" is used loosely. When you think of the act of writing, you picture someone with a pen in their hand or a computer keyboard in front of them. And some of that type of writing does take place. But the actual method of how a script gets completed is completely different (or it was back then). The writers sat around in a room and threw out ideas. A secretary took down everything that was said, and her transcription became the script.

I met the actors, most of whom were young as they were playing college students. The cast also included a housekeeper, who was a mature woman, and an older gentleman who was a love interest for me. I'd insisted on that. I refused to be cast as the old biddy. The students in my boardinghouse weren't going to have all the fun!

It turned out that our first night out in LA was Oscar night, and since the awards were broadcast on ABC, Pierre and I got to go. I've walked down many red carpets, but walking down the red carpet at the Oscars is quite another matter.

"Dr. Ruth, Dr. Ruth!" My name was called from every direction.

"Dr. Ruth, how come you're at the Oscars?" asked one reporter after the other.

"I'm shooting a pilot for ABC."

"Is it about sex?"

"No, it's a sitcom. I play a college professor."

Next. In Hollywood, during what's called pilot season, everyone is shooting a pilot.

But for me, it was daunting. I can think fast on my feet, but as for memorizing lines and then saying them with the right inflection, that's not so easy for me. On our first day on the set, we rehearsed in the morning; then in the afternoon, the cast ran through the script, reading our lines for the most part. (Actually, I was reading my lines entirely, though some of the real actors had memorized some of theirs.) The audience was composed of Fred Silverman, some other producer types, some network executives, and the writers—who made a point of laughing uproariously at each joke, not so much to show how brilliant they were but rather to give positive feedback to their cast. When we were done, the writers, including Pierre, disappeared. This was about five in the afternoon.

I went back to the Beverly Hills Hotel and waited. And waited. And waited. No word from Pierre or anyone else. Wasn't I the star of this show? How could they leave me in the dark like this? It couldn't be good news. I was certain that when I did hear from somebody, it was going to be to tell me that I was terrible, so I started to pack my bags. I was thinking to myself, "Maybe I can make a redeye home." At the very least I would leave on the first flight back to New York in the morning. At about ten p.m. the phone rang. It was Pierre.

"I don't need to hear the bad news. I'm packing my bags."

"What are you talking about?" Pierre asked.

"I haven't heard from you in five hours, so I suppose the show is kaput."

"No, we were rewriting the script. That's how it's done. The writers listen to how it goes, figure out what jokes work and which ones don't, and then they rewrite lines."

"So they're not upset with me?"

"No, not at all. They're very happy."

"We need to talk. Did you eat?" I asked Pierre.

"No."

"Then come pick me up. Let's go to Spago."

Spago is a restaurant owned by Wolfgang Puck, who is Austrian; every time I go to his restaurant, he comes over and we speak German. He also sends over his signature smoked-salmon pizza to start. The place is always jammed and it's a little hard to talk, but it's the type of atmosphere I love, particularly after having spent so many hours in my hotel room stewing.

Pierre explained what had gone on with the writers as they made adjustments. He was having a bit of a hard time contributing—even though he's written over twenty books with me and thus is a facile writer—doing it verbally, on the fly, took some getting used to for him. What he ended up doing was not paying attention to the page they were on but instead flipping ahead a few pages to see if he could come up with a joke that he would then contribute when they'd turn to the right page.

And that's how it went for more than a week. The actors would rehearse in the morning and afternoon. We'd then perform for Fred, the writers, and network executives in the late afternoon on the set that they'd built on a soundstage. The writers would all laugh like crazy at the jokes they'd written and then off they'd go to do rewrites. Then at about three in the morning, a new script would be shoved under the door to my hotel room, as if I could possibly memorize it before the next day's rehearsal.

At the end of the week we taped the episode in front of a live audience. I thought it went well, and when it aired, we won our time slot. But the big shots had first shown it to focus groups, and there it hadn't done so well. That's what did the show in.

Was I terribly upset that this experience ended in failure? To tell you the truth, no. I didn't want to move out to Los Angeles for half the year to shoot a sitcom. Yes, I could have made a lot of money, but money doesn't fascinate me as much as leading an interesting life. And in LA, working long hours to shoot a show ends up being boring. As I said earlier, my desire to be on television was to educate, not to make people laugh. I have nothing against laughter, mind you. I cannot stress it enough: the Talmud says that a lesson taught with humor is one retained, and if I can make my students laugh, I know that they'll remember what I said. But a sitcom rarely carries an educational message. And if I had ended up starring in a sitcom, I bet I never would have ended up teaching at Yale and Princeton. Yes, my wallet might have been fatter, but in my opinion I would have been poorer.

You know the saying, "The love of money is the root of all evil." Money is very important, especially having enough for the bare necessities. But look closely at the lives of poorer people—you'll see that many have more joie de vivre than those much richer than they are. That's because money can also get in the way of joie de vivre. Let's say you're going to visit a foreign country. If you stay in a luxury hotel and dine only in the finest restaurants, you'll never get a realistic picture of the country you're visiting. But if you rent a small house and shop in the markets next to the local citizens and talk to your neighbors, even if you can't speak the language, you'll appreciate where you are so much more. So I want you to have plenty of money, but I also want you to have a sense of joie de vivre so that the money doesn't dull your senses to all the enjoyment that the simple life has to offer.

Rubber Dress

This story also took place in Los Angeles, and I suppose it too could have ended my academic career—but luckily, Madonna's breasts saved the day.

I was asked to take part in an AIDS fund-raiser. Because AIDS is considered a sexually transmitted disease (though drug users can also transfer it via shared needles), when the epidemic was at its height, I felt that it was my duty to do what I could to combat this killer. That it was affecting gays more than any other group—and that I care deeply about everybody's freedom to express their sexuality— also made me want to put a little extra effort into this campaign. And so I agreed. But to tell you the truth, I hadn't really understood what I was agreeing to.

The event was a Jean Paul Gaultier fashion show, with various celebrities modeling the clothes, I didn't know much about fashion or anything about Gaultier, and I never would have imagined the outfit that he cooked up for me. This wasn't a fashion show, where the object is to sell the designer's clothes, so much as an entertainment event. Jean Paul wanted to push the envelope to keep the crowd gasping as each new celebrity came out. And what did he think the perfect look would be for me? A black rubber nurse's outfit. It had a little rubber hat and a large white bib with a red cross on it. It was the type of costume I wouldn't have felt comfortable wearing to a Halloween party, much less to parade in front of a theater full of people with the press in attendance snapping away. But I'd agreed, and I didn't find out what I would be wearing until the day before the event, when it was too late to have him come up with something else. My only other option would have been to pull out altogether, and that would have gotten me more bad press than the outfit.

When I went to the theater for the fitting, I was aghast. But here I was in front of this world famous designer, so what could I say? He was very attentive to me, putting pins here and there to make sure that it would fit just right the next night. Since he's French, we spoke in French a lot. I let common sense take a back seat and decided to let the chips land where they may. I knew that when I came out, I would get a huge reaction from the crowd, so I just told myself to have fun and hope they'd raise a lot of money for AIDS research.

Backstage the next night was quite a scene. The other celebrity models included Madonna, Raquel Welch, Faye Dunaway, Billy Idol, and Patti LaBelle, but there were also a lot of regular runway models, and they were strutting around half-naked—and in some cases totally naked. Jean Paul rushed from one celebrity to the next to make sure that their outfits would make the sensation he'd planned. With all the commotion that was going on backstage, under normal circumstances little me would have gotten lost, but once I put on my rubber dress, everyone was coming up to say how great I looked. I was thinking to myself that what they probably meant was how outlandish I looked. However, I maintained a positive attitude and tried to take some comfort in the compliments—and the fact that I was in Los Angeles and not in New York with any friends or family in the audience.

I was in the wings watching Raquel Welch strut her stuff on stage, knowing that I would be next. "Ruth," I said to myself, "you wanted to be in show business, so just make the best of it. You'll never be looked at as a serious academic again, but if some of the money raised here tonight saves even one life, then it's worth it." As I awaited my cue, I felt like someone standing on the edge of a cliff getting ready to make a very long plunge into the cold Pacific. As Raquel left the stage she gave me a big smile. Then it was my turn to walk out.

As soon as the crowd saw me, they started to scream. It was a mostly gay audience, and they don't hold anything back. If Jean Paul had wanted to get them excited at seeing this little sex therapist, he'd succeeded. I smiled, walked around the stage as I'd been instructed, answered a few questions that Jean Paul asked me, and then headed back for the wings. The press had taken hundreds of pictures in the short time I was out there, and I could just see myself on the front pages of the New York tabloids in my rubber suit.

A few other celebrities did their thing, but Jean Paul had saved Madonna for last. When I saw her backstage, I thought to myself, "For me he makes a rubber nurse's outfit, but Madonna he dresses rather sedately. Oh, well." Of course, the crowd went wild for Madonna. After all, she was one of their idols. But then the volume increased, because what I hadn't known was that she and Jean Paul had planned that she would take that sedate top off—and there was nothing underneath. So there she was, parading around with her breasts exposed. Now the photographers really went wild. Typically I wouldn't have been all that interested in seeing Madonna's breasts, but in this instance they made me smile from ear to ear, because I knew immediately that Dr. Ruth in her rubber dress had just been pushed off the front pages. If I was lucky, nobody outside of those in the theater would see me in my costume at all. It didn't turn out that way, as *People* ran a whole story on the show and included a shot of me as Nurse Rubber Fetish. But all of the attention remained focused on Madonna's nudity so that even though I had my picture shown, it didn't make a lasting impression.

In that instance, it was the paparazzi that I was worried about. Today it's not just celebrities but everybody who should be concerned about how they might be portrayed to the outside world—intentionally or not. Because the Internet has become so much a part of most people's daily lives, people treat it like the air they breathe, without thinking. But the Internet and all these electronic means of communication can have their dark side, and you must keep that in mind when using them, because the consequences can be serious. If you take compromising "selfies," you need to understand that you may not have control over where that image ends up. Personally, my attitude is that if your naked body is seen by thousands because of a cell phone hacker or malicious leak, in the end the same thing could have happened if you'd visited a nude beach. Nudity needn't be that big a deal. But if a picture of you doing something more compromising or even illegal gets around, you might never get a decent job again. Now, that's a consequence you want to avoid at all costs.

~

I am not going to defend hitchhiking. I know there's the risk that one can get picked up by the wrong person and end up a statistic. However, I also think that the average psychopath looking to pick up a young girl or boy isn't going to stop for a short, older sex therapist who might just talk him out of his mania. And it's not that I do it for kicks (at least not most of the time!), but out of necessity.

I don't know about other cities, but in New York, during the late afternoon rush hour when you're heading off to some opening or cocktail party and so many worker bees are heading home, all the cabs go off duty. You'll be standing on a corner looking to hail a cab and there will be hundreds of them passing you, all with their off-duty signs on. It's so frustrating. And I would use stronger language than "frustrating" if it happens to be raining! You can try to call for car service or use Uber or whatever, but since everyone else has the same thought, you'll be told there's a forty-five-minute wait. And I don't like to wait for anything for forty-five seconds—forget forty-five minutes. So I'm standing on a corner, there's not an available taxi in sight, and some car driver opens his window and shouts out over the traffic noise: "Hey, Dr. Ruth!" They're just being friendly, but little do they know what that open window represents to me. I go over to the car and with a big smile say, "Which direction are you heading?" If they're going anywhere near where I am, I say, "Can you give me a lift?" They're a bit shocked, but they know—as I know—that this will make a great story to tell over the water cooler: "You'll never guess who I gave a lift to!" And if they have a partner, they may even be able to weave the story into one that might lead to a sexual episode. So while they may hesitate a second, as the wheels inside their brain turn, something clicks, and they open their door . . . and I've hitchhiked once again. I've been picked up by fancy limos and cars where the driver had to throw a dozen old coffee containers into the backseat. But as long as I can get to where I'm going, I don't care. I don't think many celebrities consider it a perk of fame to be able to hitchhike when in need, but I do.

Once I was in Los Angeles with Pierre. We were staying at the Beverly Hills Hotel, which is just off Rodeo Drive—the residential part, not the strip with all the shops. We'd said we were going to walk to the shops, but when we got to the corner and were waiting for the light to cross Sunset Blvd, there was a Jeep waiting for the light to change. The driver spotted me and waved. I walked over to him and said, "Can you give us a lift?" and he said, "Sure." We hopped in, Pierre shaking his head; he hadn't hitchhiked since he was a teenager. The kicker to this story was that the Jeep driver was an Israeli. Next thing you know, we're babbling in Hebrew, which really left Catholic Pierre in shock.

The irony of these escapades is that if my children knew, they'd scold me. (Now that I've written about my wandering thumb, I suppose I'll have to promise never to do it again—a promise I'm unlikely to keep.) Having been forced to take full responsibility for myself at age ten, I have this feeling that I don't have to listen to anybody. And I don't see hitchhiking in mid-Manhattan as all that risky. If I were out in the country somewhere, I'd be a lot more careful because there are people out there who prey on hitchhikers. But so few people hitchhike in New York City that I don't really see it as taking much of a risk.

I can't end a chapter on taking risks without at least mentioning the one risk I'm always advising people not to take, risky sex. I never use the phrase "safe sex," because other than masturbation, I don't believe such a thing exists. Many people who have a sexually transmitted disease (STD) aren't aware they have one, so even if you ask someone whether they're disease free, their answer may be worthless. And condoms don't protect against all STDs; they also can break or fall off. So you can reduce the risk and have *safer* sex, but not eliminate the risk altogether. Does that stop people from having sex? Of course not. And plenty of people have sex without taking any precautions, and suffer the consequences. So please be daring—but also be careful.

I hope this chapter encourages you to take some risks, such as asking someone for a date if you don't have a partner. But I also want you to be as safe as possible, so pick and choose when to take a risk and when to play it safe.

CHAPTER X

Recognize That It Is Never Too Late

One of my attorney friends, John Silberman, once sent me a package. Since it wasn't my birthday or any other special day, I stared at it for a minute or so wondering what he could have sent me. I shook it but didn't hear anything. It was not in character for him to be sending me something out of the blue, so I had this feeling you get as you're winding the handle of a jack-in-the-box. I unwrapped it to find, of all things, two knitting needles and some wool. Not only do I not knit, but I would never sit still long enough to learn such a craft—and John clearly knows that, so this gift was getting odder and odder. There was a little envelope in the box. I lifted it out, opened it, and found a note inside that read: "If being Dr. Ruth is getting to be too much of a bother, I offer you these needles and this wool so you can retire and have something to do as you sit in a rocking chair all day long." I laughed very hard when I read that note. I guess I'd been complaining to John about something or other, and that gave him this gift idea. And it did teach me a lesson: not to complain about the responsibilities of being Dr. Ruth, especially in front of John!

I was about seventy or so when that incident took place, and now I'm eighty-six, an age at which I realize many people might have put their work life aside and taken up knitting or some other rocking chair–appropriate activity. But not me.

Sherry Lansing, who was the first woman to head a major motion picture studio and is a friend, coined the phrase, "Don't retire, rewire," and I've made it my motto. I no longer can do quite everything I once did, but I still make sure my daily schedule is full to the brim. And if there are some things I can no longer do, I substitute others. So I'm not actually slowing down; I'm just taking a route that perhaps has a few less hills, though it continues to lead me down some off-the-beaten paths.

Last year my friend Gary Tinterow called to offer one such detour. For many years he'd been a highly respected curator at the Metropolitan Museum of Art, and he coauthored *The Art of Arousal* with me. Recently he'd made a big change himself, accepting the position of director of the Museum of Fine Arts in Houston.

"Ruth, I'm putting together a lecture series here at the museum, and I want you to be my first major speaker."

"Of course, Gary. And you'll be up on stage with me."

"Naturally. We'll relive old times, discussing *The Art of Arousal*."

That book featured classic paintings involving sex that Gary had chosen and which had been paired with my comments.

"Fabulous," I said. "When do you want to do this?"

"June fourth."

That date stopped me in my tracks. June 4 is my birthday—and this was going to be my eighty-fifth birthday, which is one of those milestone years that seem to require a celebratory exclamation point. Did I want to spend my eighty-fifth birthday away from New York and all my family and friends? Certainly my children wouldn't be pleased on hearing this news. But in the split second these thoughts raced through my mind, I also considered how much fun I would have announcing to one and all that on my eighty-fifth birthday I was going to Houston for a paying gig. To me that would be the best birthday present of all, and so I gave Gary an enthusiastic yes.

When I told Pierre, he hemmed and hawed a bit and then said, "Ruth, I didn't want to tell you this, but Miriam and I have been working on a surprise birthday party for you."

"Sorry, but tell Miriam I'm going to Houston. My mind is made up, and that's that."

I can't begin to explain how delighted this turn of events made me. For the next few months, I made sure to tell everyone I ran into that instead of having a birthday party, I was going to Houston to give this lecture. This particular birthday celebration brought a smile to my face each time I thought of it. Why? Because I was upsetting the apple cart. I wasn't behaving like an eighty-five-year-old, accepting that the passing years were slowing me down. As I see it, slowing down only leads to stopping; this gig was a sign that I was going full steam ahead.

A few years ago, I had a health scare. I came down with a nagging cough, which led me to take a lot of sugary cough drops and cough medicine to control it, and that sent my blood sugar skyrocketing. Doctors had told me that my sugar was a little high, but no one had called me a diabetic, so I never imagined that taking what are essentially over-the-counter medications could land me in a hospital. But that's what happened. A week later I was scheduled to cross the Atlantic on the *Queen Elizabeth*, one of those give-a-lecture-in-exchange-for-passage deals I mentioned earlier. I started feeling better very quickly, but nobody wanted me to go on that ship. The doctors who were caring for me ordered me to stay home. A close friend who is a gynecologist did all he could to convince me not to go. My children were mad at me for even thinking about going. I was better, but they were all afraid that if I had a relapse I'd be out in the middle of the ocean—and then what? But I was adamant that I wasn't going to let this little setback upset my travel plans. So when the ship left port, I was on it. And by the time I arrived on the other side of the Atlantic, I was fit as a fiddle.

Did I board that ship out of joie de vivre or hardheadedness? To arrive at that answer, to understand how I operate, you have to look backward. I've had some narrow escapes with death but my parents and other family members weren't so lucky. To some extent, I feel as if I am living life not just for myself but for all of those who passed away. So do I have the luxury of frittering away time recovering from a cough-drop overdose? Not this orphan of the Holocaust. And had that boat gone without me, I might also have been kept from going to Israel by "doctor's orders," and that was a slippery slope that I intended to not even peer down.

They say life is short. What most people mean by that is if there's something you don't want to do—for example, accept a dinner invitation with a boring couple—you shouldn't do it. But that's the negative way of looking at a short life. I prefer to take a more positive outlook. If an interesting opportunity comes along, then I'm not going to duck behind some excuse like being too busy or tired or sick to miss out on whatever it is. At my age, life is only getting shorter, so that means now I have to cram in as much as I can. But no matter what your age, your life is getting shorter too—so don't pass up any opportunity to live it to the fullest!

By the way, accepting that offer to speak in Houston didn't mean that I missed out on my surprise party. The play about my life, *Becoming Dr. Ruth*, was set to open in Hartford a few weeks after my birthday. It had already had a run in the Berkshires, but then the playwright, Mark St. Germain, had cut it from two acts to one, and before it opened in New York, it was going to have a run in Hartford. Naturally I would be there. Cough drop-bearing wild horses couldn't have kept me away. Miriam arranged for about thirty or so friends to drive up to Hartford to a brunch before the first matinee performance. When I arrived at the theater, I didn't have to act surprised. That all these people would have traveled for so many hours just to wish me happy birthday was both amazing and touching. So you see, I got to give the lecture, collect my check, and still get a surprise party. Pulling something like that off is another Westheimer maneuver.

～

One activity I gave up with a certain amount of sadness was skiing. After I turned eighty, I decided it wasn't safe. A famous Olympic skier who is a friend of mine, Stein Eriksen, had gotten into a serious ski accident and I thought to myself, if he could get so badly injured, then what was I still doing schussing down ski slopes at my age? So I gave my skis to my granddaughter, Michal, and while I was sad, it also made me happy to know that she'd be using them.

In the days when I was still skiing, I was invited to celebrity ski invitationals at various resorts such as Vail and Banff. One of these was held at Park City, Utah, where Stein was based. I had just gotten off the lift and was at the top of the mountain when he came flying toward me, snow scattering everywhere as he skidded to a stop.

"Dr. Ruth, my favorite skiing sex therapist. Welcome to Park City. Come on, let's show these Yankees how we Europeans go down mountains."

"Sorry, Stein, I'm not in your league."

"Don't tell me you're afraid of skiing with me."

"You're too good a skier—I don't want to slow you down."

Instead of taking no for an answer, Stein ordered me to take off my skis, bent down, and had someone hoist me up on his back. Then he took off down the mountain with me holding on for dear life. As the scenery rushed by and other skiers started shouting greetings to us, we made quite a sight, me in my white ski outfit desperately hanging on to this handsome Nordic god of skiing. I was both exhilarated and terrified. Stein was undoubtedly very careful, though of course he didn't have any poles to balance himself, as his hands were holding on to my legs. I may have been safer on the back of an Olympic gold medalist than I would have been going down on my own, but at the time I was saying to myself, "Ruth Westheimer, you've had a good life, and if this is how it ends, so be it."

Giving up skiing isn't the only accommodation I've made to growing older. I hate waiting, especially at airports. In the past, in order to cut my waiting time, I would often arrive just in time to make my flight. Of course, all the additional airport screening since 9/11 has forced me to get there early. I no longer want to be nervous about missing a flight, so now when I'm going somewhere, I make sure to give myself plenty of leeway. But sometimes that's not possible. If you have a connection to make—and especially if the first leg of your journey is delayed for some reason—then when you're trying to make the next leg of your flight you have to go dashing through the airport the way OJ Simpson used to do in those Hertz commercials. That, to me, was like an accident waiting to happen. These days, if I know I have to make a connection, I ask for a wheelchair. Some of the distances you have to traverse in airports are so long, I'd rather rely on younger legs to get me there. And rather than feel this to be a loss of independence, I just sit back and enjoy the ride.

I know there are many people who feel that making an accommodation—be it to age or whatever else life throws at you—lessens joie de vivre. That certainly is true when it comes to sex. Many people think that if sex with their partner doesn't take place spontaneously that there's something wrong. But with the hectic schedules that so many couples have, planning for sex, making dates at specific times of the day, may be the only way to actually have sex. So while I'm all for spontaneous sex, I'm also for planned sex—because planned sex is far better than no sex at all.

To have joie de vivre, you not only have to be adaptable, but you also have to take on the right attitude. If you've made dinner plans and they fall through you can sulk, you can waste the evening watching TV, or you can be creative and make alternate plans. For example, take yourself to the local multiplex and see a movie. Or go to a local book store and buy the latest best seller or a book you've been meaning to read for years. Or get takeout and call your college roommate whom you haven't seen in years. Make use of that free time that's suddenly dropped in your lap instead of watching it go down the drain.

~

I've not allowed the passing years to pin me down in any way. And if there's one story that illustrates that more than any other, it's the changes I permitted, or encouraged, Nate Berkus to make in my personal habitat.

To set this story up properly, I have to tell you a bit about my apartment in Washington Heights. I've lived there for over fifty years. Since I'm not a minimalist but rather more of a pack rat, I have a history of allowing far too much stuff to pile up, literally. And since my late husband shared the same collecting habit, at times our apartment would look like a silo after a record-breaking harvest. I had a big pile of books and papers in the living room that I covered with a blanket and called my summer ski slope. Every once in a while I'd go through this pile and toss or give away large amounts of it, but I was always so busy that finding the time to make these purges was difficult—and I would never let anybody else do it, as something that I really needed might then wind up disappearing.

To compound the problem, I have two traits that add a level of difficulty to my tossing ability. One is that if I appear in a publication, I don't ask for one copy, but ten or maybe even twenty copies. I give a lot of them away to friends and family, but a lot manage to find a permanent home under my roof. And then I don't like to throw anything in the garbage that has my picture on it. I'm not usually very superstitious, but this falls into that category to some extent. So as the years went by, the amount of stuff that I wouldn't throw away grew and grew. Don't get me wrong; it never got as bad as those people you see on *Hoarders*. But conditions did get out of hand for months at a time until I was able to devote some hours to reducing the pile.

When a producer from Nate Berkus's show called Pierre, it had nothing to do with the state of my apartment. They wanted me on as a guest because of my expertise, they said. I didn't get it. He's an interior designer, and his show was all about decorating, not sex. I know less about decorating than I do about singing, so what was my role going to be on a show like that? My first reaction was to say no thank you. But then they explained what they wanted to Pierre, and he in turn told me it was an important national show. And so a date was set for me to appear.

The premise was that a woman had written to Nate saying that she and her boyfriend had broken up, and since the time he left the apartment they'd shared, she couldn't have sex there anymore because it just didn't feel right. She told her sad story on the air, then they brought me out. The studio audience gasped because they had no greater expectation of seeing me on *The Nate Berkus Show* than I'd had of being there. After I greeted Nate, I cut right to the chase.

"My dear, the answer to your question is simple: get rid of all your bedroom furniture. I understand that it evokes memories of the good and bad times you had with your boyfriend. That's not an uncommon reaction. And I understand that it might be expensive to replace it all, but you can't allow a bedroom set to ruin your sex life. So if you can't sell it, then give it away and get new furniture as soon as possible. And even if you have to sleep on a mattress on the floor for a little while, it will be worth getting your sex life back."

But while the cameras were still turning, I decided to float a trial balloon.

"Nate, I fixed this young woman's problem—now maybe you can fix mine."

"Dr. Ruth, if I can, sure."

"I've lived in my apartment for more than fifty years. I've accumulated so much junk that I'm ashamed to have anyone over, and especially not a man. Can you help me?"

Nate didn't hesitate. "Of course. We'll redecorate your apartment."

"For free?"

"Yes, for free."

I started clapping my hands with joy like guests on game shows do. I was about to get a free apartment makeover. Talk about a Westheimer maneuver!

The first step was that Nate came to visit me in my apartment. I did some cleaning up before he arrived, since he was there with a film crew to tape the "before" portion for his show and I didn't want my place to make me look like a bag lady. But the task was rather too large for me and my housekeeper to make more than a dent. I didn't know very much about Nate but when he kissed the mezuzah that was attached to the frame of my front door, I knew at least that he was Jewish, and that made me like him even more.

With the video cameras rolling, we went over my living room, and I pointed out to him why this or that item was important to me.

"I collect turtles," I explained to him when he saw all the little turtles I have everywhere. "For a turtle to survive, it has to stick its neck out. It has to take a risk. And since that's my philosophy, I like having them around me to give me courage whenever I feel the urge to crawl back into my shell."

"But you have so many."

He was right; I must have had a hundred. It may seem like I'm obsessed with them, but really it's not my fault.

"I don't buy them, people give them to me. And then I can't just throw them away, can I? But some mean more to me than others."

Nate spotted the one turtle I have whose value puts it above the level of a tchotchke, proving that he's truly an expert, even in the world of ceramic reptiles.

A week or two after Nate's visit, some of his crew came and began to pack up my belongings in plastic boxes to put in storage, each one carefully labeled. They were redoing only the front rooms, so I was able to move a lot of belongings into a spare bedroom. Eventually I did throw out or give away boxes and boxes of books and other items, but at least I could do it on my timetable. And now I'm much more careful about limiting the amount of junk that I gather (though I'll admit perfection in this skill set continues to elude me).

When it was finally time for the actual remodeling work to begin, I moved to the Waldorf Astoria Hotel. I can't say that residing in the lap of luxury particularly made me miss my apartment. On the contrary—I immediately started plotting on how I could move there permanently.

Nate's production staff had said they'd only need a couple of days to finish up. Of course, they'd been inside my apartment measuring and taking pictures in the prior weeks and much of the work, the purchasing and building of furniture, and so on, had been done ahead of time and off-site. But it took a little longer than planned. When I was asked to spend one more night at the Waldorf, I didn't complain; it seemed to me it would take a miracle to turn what I had left behind into anything that could compete with the Waldorf. But I was wrong.

The big morning, I was raring to go. The TV cameras were in front of me as I got off the elevator and rushed down my hallway toward the apartment. I tried to slow down, as the cameraman was walking backward and I didn't want him to fall. But I didn't slow down all that much because I was dying to see what had been done. They filmed me ringing the doorbell and then I had to wait a moment or two as the camera crew went inside and set up to film me as I walked through the door. I was on pins and needles, in part because I am always an impatient person, but in this case, I was especially eager to see what had become of the place I'd been calling home for over fifty years.

Nate answered the door, but he wouldn't let me in.

"Dr. Ruth, you have to close your eyes."

"But I want to see what you've done."

"Just for a second, dear, you can do it."

"All right." And so I closed my eyes and let Nate guide me into the foyer and point me so that when I opened them, I'd see my new living room.

"OK, you can open them." I did, and I looked around in utter amazement. I never would have recognized it as my old apartment. The transformation was miraculous. I was speechless, and then I started to cry. Really, on national television. I collect dollhouses and to see my cramped and crowded apartment turned into a dream dollhouse was just incredible.

I call myself a kibbutznik, which means someone who lives on a kibbutz and is more concerned with the community as a whole than him- or herself. A kibbutznik doesn't care very much about her surroundings. But saying you're a kibbutznik when you haven't lived on a kibbutz in half a century is a bit of a stretch. It's a way of saying, "What my apartment looks like is not that important to me," when what you really mean is, "I could never put together an apartment that could be in a magazine." But what I couldn't have pulled off, Nate and his crew did. And it really got to me.

But another reason I was so emotional was that many of the belongings that filled my apartment were those that my late husband, Fred, and I had purchased as a team. It's not the four walls that make up a domicile so much as what is within those four walls. And now not only was Fred no longer there. The whole front of the apartment had been stripped bare of the life we had built together, replaced by what I would call a fairy tale—because what I was staring at was a transformation that you might see in a dream but never in real life. It's not that Nate removed every trace of what was there before. Far from it. He did an incredible job of highlighting some of the items that were most precious, such as pictures of my family and other mementos, many of which had been hidden away among all the clutter. But the bottom line was that when I walk into my living room today, it's not the living room that had been created over those fifty years.

I know that there are those who change their furniture the way other people change clothes. They say it's time to redecorate, and out goes the old and in comes the new. But I'm not like that. I lost everything in the war—the only thing I have left is a wash rag with my initials embroidered onto it—and so having gone through so much loss my tendency is to hold on to everything. In my life, change had been anything but a positive experience. So asking Nate to come in and make alterations had not been an easy decision. But once I'd made it, I stuck to it, and am I glad I did.

Let me highlight two of the many changes Nate made. First, everyone I knew had a flat-screen TV except me. It's not that I couldn't have afforded one, but where would I have put it? I don't know how he moved all the wiring to the opposite wall from where my little set had resided, but now I have a flat-screen TV hanging in my living room. I don't watch a lot of TV, but when I do, I always thank Nate for the view!

The other thing he did was to make some of the furniture my size. I usually manage with regular-size furniture, but I'm not totally comfortable. Now I have chairs that fit *me* rather than chairs *I* have to fit into. So you see, Nate really did design this apartment for me, not for the TV show or some designer magazine. He studied me and set out to create a home that I would love. And he succeeded. And

I took a chance by asking Nate. Now my home no longer looks like that of an eighty-six-year-old woman but instead is a sleek, modern residence that could belong to someone half my age!

~

In Israel there's a lot of group singing and dancing that goes on, and when I lived there, I never missed a chance to take part. These social activities were the reward for hours spent under the hot Israeli sun, filling up baskets with olives or grapes. But when your voice is mixed in with those of a lot of others, it's not that obvious that you can't hold a tune. However, when you're the only one singing, your deficiencies become a lot more apparent, which is why as soon as my children were old enough to speak their mind, they forbade me from singing another note in their presence. So the fact that I was once up for a Grammy Award came as quite a surprise, most of all to me. And that my singing "career" didn't begin until I was in my seventies shows that one should never say never.

An award wasn't in the offing the first time I sang in public—just a bad case of nerves. I was asked to take part in a special performance of the show *Pippin* to raise money to combat AIDS. It was a concert version, meaning different celebrities would appear just to sing the songs of the show. There's one tune in that show that was made famous on Broadway by the character actress Irene Ryan, "No Time at All." The words of that song can actually be spoken, and that's what I was supposed to do, backed up by four good-looking hunks to sing the chorus and cavort around me.

The offer to do this came through Merle Frimark, with whom Pierre shared an office at the time.

"Dr. Ruth, you have to do this. We're raising money to fight AIDS, and your name on the program will be important."

"But Merle, I can't sing, and everyone else will be famous singers."

"You won't have to really sing. You just have to speak the words to the right beat. All the victims of AIDS need you there."

I was pushed into acquiescing, but to say I had reservations is putting it mildly. It wasn't a case of typical stage fright. By that point I'd done hundreds of lectures in front of huge crowds. (I actually put in my lecture contract that I won't speak in front of crowds bigger than three thousand because I'd done a couple like that and didn't like not being able to connect with the audience.) What I had was zero confidence in my ability to sing, even in a talking style.

When I do a commercial, I tell those in charge that I call myself "One-Take Westheimer" and I never want to rehearse because I feel it spoils the spontaneity of my performance. (I always give them as many takes as they like, but I don't want them to know that or we'd be there all day.) But for this show, I insisted that there be a lot of rehearsals. I went to the director's studio half a dozen times, and we went over the song again and again.

"Dr. Ruth, that was perfect."

"No, it wasn't. I was terrible."

"Really, you were great. And remember, you'll have the four guys backing you up."

"But they won't be doing my part. They'll be doing the chorus."

"Trust me, the audience is going to love you."

I didn't trust him at all. Normally when I do something in public, I let all my family and friends know about it. This time I told Pierre I didn't want anybody I knew in the audience. If I was going to make a complete fool of myself, I didn't want friends or family as witnesses. The only two people who saw my musical debut were Pierre and his wife, Joanne. And what they saw was me getting a standing ovation! Every time I started to walk off stage, the audience roared even louder, so I had to go back out and take another bow.

Of course, I later regretted not having invited those children of mine who never wanted to hear me sing. Imagine how I would have been able to gloat over the reaction I got from that audience. Oh, well—at least I didn't chicken out and was able to bask in the glow of that standing ovation for a little while.

The next person to approach me to sing was Tom Chapin. Tom, the brother of the late Harry Chapin, specializes in children's music and he wrote a song, "Two Kinds of Seagulls," about the fact that animals come in pairs—he-gulls and she-gulls, for example. Though the song was very cute, I don't know if I would have agreed to join Tom in a duet if I hadn't been in the *Pippin* event. But that show gave me more confidence—and since we'd be recording in a studio, not in front of a live audience, I didn't have to be One-Take Westheimer but could afford to muff my lines.

Tom is very tall and I'm very short, but the engineer was able to work out the mike situation in the studio easily. Tom and I have performed this song together in front of an audience a few times, once even at Carnegie Hall, and in order for it to work, what he ends up doing is going down on his knees. So you have a funny song and a funnier-looking couple, and audiences eat it up. Tom deserves all the credit for writing such a cute little ditty and then being smart enough to ask me to join him. And the album the song was on, *This Pretty Planet*, got nominated for a Grammy, further proof of Tom's talents.

Not long after that, a woman I'd met once in a chocolate shop and to whom I'd given Pierre's contact information started bugging Pierre about wanting me to narrate some fairy tales. She was part of a classical music group, An die Musik; the concept she had was that they would play original music to accompany the fairy tales that I would read. I hesitated for a while, but I had young grandchildren at the time whom I felt would like to have a CD of fairy tales read by their *omi*, so I decided to at least explore the possibility.

Connie Emmerich is a very distinguished-looking, gray-haired woman with a large apartment on Fifth Avenue who talks very, very fast. I move fast, but because I tend to enunciate what I say, I actually speak rather slowly. (Whenever I do a commercial and they write copy for me, they end up having to cut it because the words won't all come out of my mouth within the allotted sixty seconds. But since it's my unique accent that they want, they have to put up with my rolled *r*'s.) Connie, however, was a speed talker; I often had to tell her to take a breath so I could follow what she was saying. But when I went to her place for tea to meet the other musicians, and she sat down at the piano, they picked up their instruments, and all played me the music that composer Bruce Adolphe had written, I was enchanted. This time there was no pretense that I was singing. All I had to do was read "Little Red Riding Hood" and "Goldilocks and the Three Bears" while they played the music in between each little scene.

"So, Dr. Ruth, what did you think? Isn't the music beautiful? It fits these fairy tales so well. I just know with you doing the narration this CD will be well received."

"Connie, you don't have to sell me anymore. I'll do it. I know my grandchildren will love it, plus it will make a terrific Hanukkah present."

What I didn't know when I agreed to be a part of this project was that the real present would be a Grammy nomination.

The opportunity to win an award like that doesn't come around very often, so I when I got the word, I went into high gear. This was in 2002; I'd written a couple of Dummies books, and the man who started the For Dummies series and signed me to write those books, John Kilcullen, was now president of *Billboard* magazine. I made an appointment to see him.

"John, you were the most important man in my life when *Sex for Dummies* came out, and now you're going to play that role again."

"Ruth, you know anything I can do for you, I will." John is a real sweetheart.

"I made an album of me reading some children's fairy tales backed by a classical music group and guess what? It's been nominated for a Grammy."

"That's terrific. We have to put together a campaign so you win."

"That's why I'm here. What are we waiting for?"

John introduced me to some of his staff members. We set up an interview for an article in the magazine, and someone took the job of designing an ad. Of course, now I had to find the funds to pay for that ad—but when I set my mind to something, it happens, and so my Grammy campaign got launched. Pierre was able to get me a lot of publicity; it's not every day that Dr. Ruth is nominated for a Grammy, so the press were very interested.

The award ceremony took place at the end of February, and I went out to LA. I stayed at my usual place, the Beverly Hills Hotel, and held court at the Polo Lounge and at the pool. I got myself invited to several parties and met some rock stars, most of whom I didn't know, but they all knew me and were big fans. My line to all of them was, "I hope you voted for me!" and they all said they did. I believed them, and the night of the actual awards, as I sat down in my seat, I felt confident that I was going to win. Can you guess who beat me out? None other than my friend Tom Chapin. Two years in a row his album was nominated, but it was the one I wasn't on that won.

"Tom, congratulations, you deserve it!" I said to him when I saw him later at the afterparty.

"Ruth, thank you. Sorry I didn't win last year; then we could have shared this award."

I really didn't begrudge Tom for winning. He's a very talented songwriter, singer, and musician, with years' worth of experience. All I had done was stick my toe in the water. But no matter how much you tell yourself winning doesn't really matter, it still hurts to lose.

I was fifty-two years old when I started my first radio show. I'd never dreamed of having a radio program, and certainly not having one that would make me world famous. So when I tell you it's never too late, I'm the living proof of that.

There are some people who always wanted to learn how to play the piano but don't start taking lessons until their children have grown. Fred Westheimer was one of those people, and he loved it. But maybe you don't yet know what new thing is going to bring added happiness into your life. Maybe you were awful in art class in elementary school; that doesn't mean you should assume that you couldn't be a painter. If you feel the itch to paint, even if you can barely do stick figures, go and take some lessons. If after a few lessons you come to the realization that you really don't have any talent in this area, then drop it. But if you make some progress and if you enjoy it, then you can have it be your hobby or maybe even turn it into a career.

There are some women who expect their sex life to wither and die once they go through menopause. With that expectation, that's exactly what happens. But there are others who come to the realization that sex without the risk of getting pregnant is better than ever. Their sex lives bloom after menopause, especially if their kids leave them with an empty nest and the added privacy that brings.

Your attitude toward life is what allows joie de vivre to flow into it. I'm not saying that you'll succeed at everything you try, but if you never try anything, then I can offer you a rock-solid guarantee that you'll never succeed at anything you didn't try!

EPILOGUE

Questions from the Audience

People love to ask me questions, and every so often I would go up on stage at the end of a performance of *Becoming Dr. Ruth* with the star, Debra Jo Rupp, and often the playwright, Mark St. Germain, and we'd go back and forth with the audience. I thought I might end this book by offering you some of the answers I gave over the run of the shows in various venues, especially those that relate to living life to the fullest.

Q: What do you do when you feel sad?

I reach into my rainy-day desk drawer. It's chock full of letters that various friends and strangers sent me over the years that made me feel good when I first read them. If I'm having a bad day, I open that drawer and pull out a couple of those letters to read to myself, and afterward, my spirits are back up to their normal level.

The key to behavioral therapy—of which sex therapy is one branch—is not to frustrate yourself attempting to stop certain thoughts or emotions from happening in the first place. If something happens to bring your spirits down or your blood pressure up, you can't stop the triggering of those negative emotions. What you can do is shorten the duration of how long they affect you. But to effectively do that, it's often useful to have some tools to push your thought pattern in another direction. That's where my rainy-day letters come in. But what you employ may be far different. Happy music, reading some jokes that you've put in a box or a file on your computer, even taking a hot shower could accomplish the same end for you. But what you use doesn't necessarily have to be external. Just by thinking about some happy memories could cause the same positive effect. It will work only if you actively turn to this method of behavioral therapy whenever your emotional response is affecting you negatively. You need to train your brain not to respond—in some cases actually crave—this negativity. After a while, you'll meet with more and more success.

Now, I wish I could teach you how to avoid unpleasant situations altogether, but as you've seen from my life, that's a talent I'm sorely lacking in. And since most people don't have any more control over their fate than I do, the key to maximizing the joie de vivre in your life is to be prepared for a case of life hiccups. If your boss says something to upset you, it's easy to dive into those negative feelings, and the deeper you dive, the harder it will be to come out of your funk. So as soon as you realize where you're heading, force yourself to think of some memories that always serve to brighten your spirit. Maybe it was a surprise birthday party that brought a huge smile to your face, or the moment you met your spouse. You shouldn't pull out a voodoo doll of your boss from your desk drawer; that won't help you wipe out any negative feelings but instead will make them that much stronger. You have to select from your own set of positive memories, and as I said, bolster them with some external life vests like letters (or printed-out e-mails), music, or whatever.

Q: On the set of the play and in your remodel with Nate Berkus, photographs seemed to be everywhere. What kind of significance do you attach to these?

Because of the Holocaust, I was left with only a few pictures of my parents instead of a whole treasure trove that would have served to remind me of happy times that we'd spent together. Their pictures are, of course, placed prominently in my apartment. Every time I look at them, I draw strength because they loved me so much, and so seeing them up on my wall sends me a message of love. The same is true of the pictures that I have of Fred, my children, and my grandchildren.

Today people take a million pictures, but because the pictures are digital, there's a good chance that they're buried deep in a hard drive or up in the cloud where you can't see them regularly. Even if you live with someone, there are days when maybe you're not getting along, but if you catch a glimpse of a picture of the two of you in a happier moment, it will change your mood. So I urge you to print some of your digital pictures and put them around your house where they can be seen. (A digital frame can do the same thing.) The same is true of printed pictures that are sitting in a closed album, by the way. Put some of them in frames, or at least leave an album or two out on your coffee table. Pictures can do wonders for your mood but you have to be able to see them.

I also have pictures of me from some special moments around my apartment. There's one of me and President Clinton. This isn't widely known, but without me, he might not have become president. OK, I'm exaggerating—but I did tell him to run when he was still only governor of Arkansas. What's special about President Clinton is the way he looks at you. You really feel that he's making a connection.

That type of connection is becoming rarer and rarer. You're with people, but they seem to spend as much time checking their messages on their phone as looking at you. If you want to live life to the utmost, it has to be with other people. The connections you make via a phone or computer just don't satisfy the way real interpersonal connections do. We humans spent millions of years evolving into being social animals, and we need other people to be complete. All this tweeting, Facebooking, and the like is a weakened form of communication. Without eye contact, touching, hearing the sound of someone's intonations, seeing the changes in their facial expressions, you lose so much of the message. To experience joie de vivre, you need a living, breathing person or people around you, not machines. And you have to concentrate on those around you and not let yourself be distracted by people connected to you only via some piece of electronic equipment.

Now, if you don't particularly like the people you're with—assuming they're not family so that you have no choice—and that's why you're constantly checking your smart phone, then find new people to be with. You can use your electronic gizmos to help you find those people, but once you're together, put those gizmos away. And remember, if a relationship isn't all that interesting, you may be partially to blame as well. How much are you investing in good conversation? Are you suggesting that you visit interesting places with your friends, or are you willing to just "hang"? Joie de vivre is not low-hanging fruit. You have to put some effort into experiencing joy and happiness. So if there is anything unsatisfying about your relationships, first see what avenues are open to making improvements. But if it turns out to be hopeless, then move on.

Q: What are some of the tools you've used to cope with the devastating losses you faced as a child?

I have five dollhouses in my living room, two of which are quite large. They're filled with furniture and other accessories, and only I get to play with them. That's right—when my grandchildren were little and wanted to play with Omi's dollhouses the answer was no.

As you already know, I lost all of my toys when I was ten. I had a friend of mine, Dr. Lou Lieberman, build me these dollhouses to order. To some extent, they're to make up for the toys I lost, but they also offer me something else. When the Nazis destroyed my family, I lost control over my fate. I was put on a train heading who knows where and then was under the direction of the people who ran the orphanage, who weren't very nice to us. When I play with my dollhouses, I am in full control. If I put a little figurine in one place, that's where it has to stay. So for me, playing with these dollhouses is a form of therapy. If the furniture and dolls were moved around haphazardly, I would feel a loss of control that would make me feel very uncomfortable. These dollhouses represent a perfect world, which the real one is not. They are not toys that I am going to outgrow, but rather tools that I use to make myself feel better when I feel that life is a little out of control.

So what tool or tools might you use that would have a similar effect? It could be something as simple as cooking. I'm not talking about merely preparing some food for dinner but planning out a meal that offers you some challenges so that when you're done, you feel that you've accomplished something worthwhile and your spirits will be lifted.

Exercise is another tool you could use. For exercise to be most profitable, you should be able to note progress. If you did twenty-five pushups yesterday, you should try to do twenty-six today. By giving yourself concrete goals—and meeting them—you'll have a source of satisfaction that is under your control.

The opposite side of this coin is the concept of vegging out. You've had a bad day, and so you sit down on the couch and watch TV. I'm not against watching TV when there's a program you want to watch, but if you turn it on just to kill time, then that's not going to really help you. Your brain is somewhat plastic and can be trained. By doing something active, you can forget your troubles. If you are inactive, then even if your troubles get pushed aside for a time, they'll pop right back as soon as you turn off that TV.

Reading, on the other hand, is a lot more active. When you read a descriptive passage, your brain has to imagine the scene and so your synapses are firing away. You are forced to concentrate so much more reading, which is active, than watching TV, which is passive. (OK, if you're watching *Jeopardy* and trying to guess the answers, you get some added brownie points.)

Again, bear in mind I'm not telling you to employ such methods once but every time the joy is getting sucked out of your life. Use these activities to help adjust your brain from negative to positive thinking. Joie de vivre doesn't just jump into your lap like a puppy. You need to put some effort into being happier.

Q: Do you really have hundreds of turtles?

My living room is filled with turtles, and as I've said before, it's because turtles have to stick their neck out to do anything. They have to take risks, and taking risks is part of embracing joie de vivre. There are good times to be had out there, but very often you have to go looking for them.

Should you fill your house with turtles? It doesn't matter what you use as a reminder to yourself; just having some symbols around can be useful. Let's say that when you were young, you took a lot of dance lessons and wanted to be a ballerina. You really enjoyed all that dancing that you did. OK, so put some little faience ballerinas around your house to remind you of those days. And each time you see one, go up on your tiptoes and twirl around. Sound silly? Who cares, as long as this action triggers certain emotions that elevate your spirits. None of this has to take a lot of time, but whatever you choose should help to focus on uplifting thoughts that will give you a psychological boost.

Many people have real pets, and it's been shown that having a pet can be therapeutic. But don't make the mistake of acting like a pet is an actual human being. Don't allow a pet to become a crutch. If someone asks you to go to dinner and you say, "Sorry, I can't, I have to go home to be with my pet," then that's a problem. I understand that your pet may need walking, feeding, and so on, but then plan ahead so that you have a neighbor who will handle such duties for you, for pay if necessary. If you're the type of person who might use a pet as an excuse, I'd tell you not to have one. Now, an older person who is housebound could absolutely have use of a pet. I don't want you to think I'm anti-pets. I just want you to be conscious of not using a pet as a crutch that will keep you isolated. I'll repeat myself: acquiring joie de vivre requires other humans, not animals.

Q: Do you collect anything else besides dollhouses and turtles?

Sigmund Freud kept a collection of ancient sculptures from Egyptian, Greek, and Roman times on his desk, and I have some replicas of those. Now, I'm not a Freudian, as I'm not a psychoanalyst but a behavioral therapist. But I admire Freud for changing the way we think about, well, thinking—what our thoughts and dreams mean. I like to say that we all stand on the shoulders of giants, those that came before us and made breakthroughs in whatever field we are in, and Freud is certainly one of the giants on whose shoulders I stand, even though I don't share his discipline. What he changed was that he made it possible to improve a person's mental state. Just having people believe that is possible makes it easier for me to get those who come to me with a sexual problem to heed my advice. If they believe I can help them, then it's much more likely that I can. And if they come in to my office with a chip on their shoulder, then I probably will fail. So Freud helped people believe that getting help with mental fitness was possible. Thus he proved a great help to all those, like myself, who've followed in his footsteps. Who inspires you? And have you maximized the possibilities of their inspiration? It could be someone you know or knew personally, such as a parent, teacher, or other mentor, or else someone you've never met but admire greatly, like I do Freud. The point is, it's very hard to create joy—or anything—from nothing. But if you have a foundation, then it becomes much easier.

To make this easier to understand, let's say you had a math teacher in high school who inspired you to work a little harder than your other teachers. It doesn't matter whether or not you actually like math or use math much today. What does matter is that this teacher drew out the best in you, even if it was only a C rather than an F. Now let's say there was an equation that you "fondly" remember from that class. Blow it up, put it in a frame, and draw inspiration from it. When you're faced with a difficult situation, remember how you conquered that equation and how this teacher elicited from you the necessary effort. If you can go into difficult tasks with more enthusiasm and self-confidence, that will bring you joie de vivre. What kills the enjoyment of life is dread. If you are constantly running from this or that task that needs to be addressed, those negative emotions will suck the life out of everything else you do. But if you have the confidence that you will come through in the end—in part because of that mathematical equation that you didn't let bring you down back in high school—then when you give a kiss to your spouse in the morning, you won't do it halfheartedly, but with joie de vivre!

If you've never thought along these lines, then maybe you think you don't have anyone in your past like that, so my first homework assignment to you is to look back and see who influenced you and in which ways. I bet that after a little pondering, you'll find several such important influences in your life. Then find ways to remind yourself of what they taught you so that you can use the light they shone on a regular basis.

Q: I watched the episode of Nate Berkus when he redid your apartment. When he arrived, he kissed something on your door frame. What was it?

A mezuzah, which contains some verses from a Jewish prayer, Shema Yisrael. Jews put it on the door frame to fulfill a mitzvah, a Biblical commandment. I have many religious symbols in my house, starting with the mezuzah as well as two menorahs (candleholders) in my living room. I feel that having religious objects around, whichever religion you practice, can help increase your joie de vivre. If you practice a religion and believe that God loves you, then any time you remind yourself of your faith, that can lift your spirits. I'm not here to push one religion—and I'm certainly not saying that if you are an agnostic or atheist that you can't experience joie de vivre. However, I do put faith in the concept that religious belief can help you to get through the tough parts of the day. And so, if appropriate, you should use your religious beliefs to lighten your burdens.

Religious belief also toughens you. Certainly we Jews have had to remain tough in order to hold on to our faith, which through history various peoples have tried to forcibly eliminate from the planet. So how does being tough add to joie de vivre? It's simple. If you're a wimp, then the least little setback will send you cowering to the corner, and you can't cower and experience the joys of life at the same time. To fully enjoy what life has to offer, you have to take risks, and that includes the risks of standing up for your religion or your country or whatever it is you believe in.

Q: How do you chase away negativity?

I have only one item left from my childhood, a washrag embroidered with my initials. You might think I'd have it on display, but instead I keep it hidden. Even after all these years, the painful memories that washrag evokes are just too powerful. I expect my grandmother packed it, so it represents the last thing she ever did for me. I can look at a picture of her and make sure that I concentrate on all the positive images the photo evokes, but I just can't seem to be able to do that with the washcloth. Seeing it brings me right back to that train ride from Frankfurt, which is the worst day in my life. I don't need to be reminded of that day, either when I'm leaving to go out into the world or coming back from a day packed with activities. It's always there in the back of my mind. For it to be front and center would quickly vacuum up all the joie de vivre I could muster.

So I would say that you should do the same: put away anything that reminds you of negative times. If your first marriage ended in a bitter divorce, then even though that wedding day was wonderful, you might not want pictures of it around. Of course, your reaction to a specific trigger is going to be very personal. You might be the type of person who can look at such a wedding picture and get inspired by how much it meant to you to have both parents there. I'm not offering a hard-and-fast rule here except to say if there's an object that always leaves you feeling down when you look at it, then don't display it.

By the way, this advice is actually what led me to get Nate Berkus to redo my apartment. As I said in chapter ten, I was asked to appear on his show to help out a young lady who was having trouble becoming aroused with a new boyfriend because the furniture reminded her of the old one; I told her to get rid of the furniture, no matter the cost. This example shows that I'm not just spouting some meaningless words when I say that objects can keep you from experiencing joy. This actually takes place all the time. And yet while the answer may seem obvious—get rid of such objects, or at least hide them—many people don't heed this commonsense approach. They'll find practical reasons to hold on to an object, such as in this case, the expense of buying new furniture that the young lady felt was stopping her. Another "reason" might be peer pressure: "You got rid of your furniture because it reminded you of Phil? What were you thinking?" If anyone says to you to do something that makes you uncomfortable, just turn away and don't pay them any mind. Only you know how to maintain the optimum control over your emotional state, and if looking at anything that stirs painful memories is too painful, then don't do it.

Q: What do you think is the biggest danger to a relationship?

Boredom. No one can feel joyful every day. There are days when something happens that just saps you of all positive feelings. It could be something major, like the death of someone close to you, and then it might take some time for that cloud to lift. It could also be something relatively minor—a nasty comment sent your way that takes a few hours to put aside. But there's an insidious force out there that, while rather mild mannered, can keep you from experiencing joie de vivre on an everyday basis, and that's boredom.

Boredom is like a fog that clings to you and, though the effects are minor, keeps you from seeing all the ways there are to enjoy life. After a while you may begin to feel that boredom is a condition that is always with you. So rather than fight it, you give in to it, accepting to live a life that lacks richness and energy.

The first step to fighting boredom is to recognize it. One clue is that you're always tired even though there's no particular cause, like a baby who wakes you five times a night or financial worries that keep you from falling asleep. The reason that you are tired is that there's nothing about your life that makes you excited. If you have nothing to look forward to, then a listless funk will surround you, and a nap becomes enticing because at least your dreams are somewhat entertaining.

If you want to experience joie de vivre, you have to actively combat boredom. Now, boredom is pretty much a wimp and doesn't usually put up much of a fight, unless you happen to live on a desert island or a cultural wasteland. Just because you don't live near Broadway or Lincoln Center doesn't mean there aren't plenty of activities near you that will stimulate your intellect. A local theater company may have amateur actors, but the play or musical will be something that probably won an award when it first came out. If there's no book club near you, start one. If there are children stuck for long periods of time in a nearby hospital, go read to them. Join a local political party and stir the pot. If you think a certain corner needs a traffic signal, collect signatures on a petition. You can even take courses at major colleges online for free. By investing in yourself in all these ways, you'll find that the fog of boredom will lift and the bright light of joie de vivre will begin to light your life.

But let's say that you're having problems getting out of a funk. Maybe your lack of joie de vivre isn't a condition you can handle on your own. Maybe you need some professional guidance. Or if you're what is called clinically depressed, some medication. If you suspect that this may be the case, then go get the help you need.

When I wrote my first autobiography, *All in a Lifetime*, I knew that I wouldn't be able to handle going over the very sad parts of my life by myself. I'd never really dealt with that period of my life, had never reread my diaries, and when my children asked me about it, I'd change the subject. But my publisher wasn't going to accept such dodges. So I went to a psychoanalyst I knew and leaned on him to dig down into myself for the truth. As I told the *New York Times*, I was afraid of losing my joie de vivre if I spent too much time delving into my past, but with a psychoanalyst's help, that didn't happen.

That story didn't appear in the *New York Times* by accident. Yes, Pierre pitched it to them, but only because I wanted that story told. I wanted my audience to know that I practiced what I preached, that when I was faced with a problem, I got professional help. And that's what I'm urging you to do. It's OK to say, "I can't handle this," but it's not OK to then do nothing about the problem. If there is help, you should avail yourself of that help.

Whatever your age, you have no idea how much time you have left, and for that reason I strongly believe that you don't have any time to waste. Even if you can't control time, you can control the quality of your life during the time you have. You don't want to come to a point in your life where you're left with nothing but a stack of regrets. Joie de vivre isn't just a phrase that you sprinkle on your life now and then. It's an attitude that should permeate your every waking hour. It takes a little effort but let me assure you, the rewards are well worth it.

Q: Is the Dr. Ruth legend coming to an end?

Radio, TV, books, the Internet, and now a play have all helped me reach out to people in order to give them some guidance. I absolutely delight in being a celebrity, but my main goal of helping people to learn remains my top priority. It's why at the age of eighty-six I keep teaching and going around the world giving lectures and coming out with new books. As far as I'm concerned, I'm still becoming Dr. Ruth.

ACKNOWLEDGMENTS

From Dr. Ruth K. Westheimer:

To the memory of my entire family who perished during the Holocaust. To the memory of my late husband, Fred, who encouraged me in all my endeavors. To my current family: my daughter, Miriam Westheimer, EdD; son-in-law Joel Einleger, MBA; their children, Ari and Leora; my son, Joel Westheimer, PhD; daughter-in-law Barabara Leckie, PhD; and their children, Michal and Benjamin. I have the best grandchildren in the entire world!

Thanks to all the many family members and friends for adding so much to my life. I'd need an entire chapter to list them all, but some must be mentioned here: Pierre Lehu and I have now collaborated on a dozen books; he's the best minister of communications I could have asked for! Cliff Rubin, my assistant, thanks!; Dr. Peter Banks; Peter Berger, MD; Simon and Stefany Bergson; Nate Berkus; David Best, MD; Chuck Blazer; Frank Chervenak, MD; Richard Cohen, MD; Martin Englisher; Cynthia Fuchs Epstein, PhD; Howard Epstein; Meyer Glaser, PhD; David Goslin,

PhD; Amos Grunebaum, MD; Dylan Hanson; Polly and Herman Hochberg; David Hryck, Esq.; Steve Kaplan, PhD; Rabbi Barry Dov Katz and Shoshi Katz; Bonnie Kaye; Patti Kenner; Robert Krasner, MD; Nathan Kravetz, PhD; Marga and Bill Kunreuther; Dean Stephen Lassonde; Matthew and Vivian Lazar; Rabbi and Mrs. William Lebeau; Robin and Rosemary Leckie; Hope Jensen Leichter, PhD; Jeff and Nancy Jane Loewy; John and Ginger Lollos; Sanford Lopater, PhD, and Susan Lopater; David Marwell; Marga Miller; Peter Niculescu; Dale Ordes; Frank and Jodi Osborn; Rabbi James and Elana Ponet, PhD; Leslie Rahl; Bob and Yvette Rose; Debra Jo Rupp; Carrie Russo; Larry and Camille Ruvo; Simeon and Rose Schreiber; Daniel Schwartz; Amir Shaviv; David Simon, MD; Jerome Singerman, PhD; Betsy Sledge; William Sledge, MD; Mark St. Germain; Henry and Sherri Stein; Jeff Tabak, Esq., and Marilyn Tabak; Malcolm Thomson; Shkurte Tonaj; Greg Willenborg; and Ilse and Max Wyler-Weil and to all the people at Amazon Publishing who worked so hard to bring this book into the world: Jeff Belle, Daphne Durham, Tara Parsons, Maggie Sivon, and the entire team, as well as Amazon's founder and his wife, Jeff and McKenzie Bezos, who helped me launch this endeavor.

From Pierre Lehu:

Thanks to my wife, Joanne Seminara, who not only provided her usual support but on this book added her legal expertise; my son, Peter, daughter-in-law, Melissa Sullivan, and fantastic grandson, Jude Sullivan Lehu; my daughter, Gabrielle, and my son-in-law, Jim Frawley; my in-laws, Joe and Anita Seminara and the entire Seminara clan.

ABOUT THE AUTHOR

Dr. Ruth K. Westheimer is a psychosexual therapist who sprang to national attention in the early 1980s with her live radio program, *Sexually Speaking*. She went on to have her own TV program, appeared on the covers of *People* and *TV Guide*, and is the author of thirty-seven books. Fans of all ages can find her at drruth.com, on Twitter (@AskDrRuth), and at YouTube.com/drruth. A one-woman show about her life, *Dr. Ruth, All The Way*, is currently touring. Dr. Ruth teaches at Columbia University's Teachers College. She lives in New York City and has two children and four grandchildren.